What people are saying about …

# Beyond the Brady

"This book is a treasure chest of encouragement, hope, and inspiration for the blended family. It has been said that some families cannot blend; they can only collide. Not true. The Alsdorf family has 'collided' well. They are the real deal and a beautiful picture of a fantastic blended family."

**Dr. Gary Smalley,** best-selling author of
*The Blessing* and *The Language of Love*

"I have had the joy of pastoring the local church where Ray and Debbie have lived out the practical lessons taught in this new book. From the day they first met me until now, this beautiful couple has learned priceless lessons about blending families that they now share with all of us. Through their example they have earned the right to teach us all."

**Steve Madsen,** lead pastor of Cornerstone
Fellowship in Livermore, CA

"With candor and heartfelt compassion, Ray and Debbie Alsdorf share the complexities and blessings they experienced when merging two homes into one. *Beyond the Brady Bunch* offers biblical wisdom and practical insights for today's stepfamily."

**Laura Petherbridge,** international speaker
and author of *When "I Do" Becomes "I
Don't"* and *The Smart Stepmom*

"My wife and I have been in a Hers, Mine, and Ours family for over twenty-five years and have lived the dynamics in this book. This book stands alone in its grip on the realities of making a blended family successful. Step-by-step, the authors walk the reader through the incredible complexities of bringing two broken families together to form a new family unit. They also tackle the importance of using biblical principles for the blended family in a realistic way. The Alsdorfs realize that having God at the center is the most important factor. Anyone already in a blended family, or entering a blended family, *must* read this book!"

**Dennis McFadden,** Marriage and Family therapist and executive pastor of Shoreline Community Church in Monterey, CA

"Ray and Debbie Alsdorf have written a powerful book addressing the issues most people shy away from. I learned an incredible amount about the challenges of blending two separate families into one. They combine raw honesty and touching humor in ways only couples who have been through war (or remarriage) together can. I am tremendously impressed by this book."

**Rick Johnson,** best-selling author of *The Man Whisperer* and *Becoming Your Spouse's Better Half*

Beyond the
Brady
Bunch

# Beyond the
# Brady Bunch

### HOPE & HELP FOR BLENDED FAMILIES

## RAY & DEBBIE ALSDORF

David C Cook®
*transforming lives together*

BEYOND THE BRADY BUNCH
Published by David C. Cook
4050 Lee Vance View
Colorado Springs, CO 80918 U.S.A.

David C. Cook Distribution Canada
55 Woodslee Avenue, Paris, Ontario, Canada N3L 3E5

David C. Cook U.K., Kingsway Communications
Eastbourne, East Sussex BN23 6NT, England

David C. Cook and the graphic circle C logo
are registered trademarks of Cook Communications Ministries.

All Scripture quotations, unless otherwise noted, are taken from the *Holy Bible,
New International Version*®. *NIV*®. Copyright © 1973, 1978, 1984 by International
Bible Society. Used by permission of Zondervan. All rights reserved.
The author has added italics to Scripture quotations for emphasis.

LCCN 2010928371
ISBN 978-1-4347-6645-8
eISBN 978-0-7814-0504-1

© 2010 Debbie and Ray Alsdorf
Published in association with the literary agency of Les
Stobbe, 300 Doubleday Rd., Tryon, NC 28782.

The Team: Terry Behimer, Karen Lee-Thorp, Amy Kiechlin,
Sarah Schultz, Caitlyn York, Karen Athen.
Cover design: Rule 29
Cover images: iStockphoto, royalty-free

Printed in the United States of America
First Edition 2010

1 2 3 4 5 6 7 8 9 10

052810

To our children,

Justin, Ashley, Cameron, and Megan—

in the end, all that counts is love for
God and love for others. You have been
our inspiration to hope in God's love,
to trust in God's power to heal, and
to hold on to God's value of family.

We love you!

# Contents

# Acknowledgments

This book was not easy to write. There were challenges every step of the way. With every project as big as the writing of a book, there are people along the way who made a difference. Here is the fun part of writing—thanking those people.

Our literary agent, Les Stobbe, and our publishers, Terry Behimer and Don Pape—thank you for believing in this project and giving us this opportunity.

Every book needs a good editor—thank you, Karen Lee-Thorp, for editing with patience, understanding, and excellence!

Our Marriage Builders Group—you are our "other" family. Where would we be without your friendships? It's hard to put into words what you mean to us, how your prayers over the years have held us up, and how your support has given us strength. We love each of you. Rich and Kim Pace, Eddie and BethAnn Moitoso, Mark and Teresa Burke, Paul and Patti Esser, Mark and Natalie Anderson, Mike and Cathy Tennyson, Gene and Cindy Williams—and of course our honorary members who moved away—Scott and Lorri Steer.

Pastor Steve Madsen for believing in blended-family ministry and wanting the blended families at Cornerstone to succeed. We appreciate you.

Caren Wolfe, for being a source of encouragement and support as you have paved the way for blended-family ministry to be part of the marriage ministry at Cornerstone Fellowship. We appreciate your leadership and your heart for marriage.

And a special thanks to Jane Jewell and Jennifer Cuellar for your administrative help with the blended-family classes at Cornerstone.

Dr. Don Partridge and Jenetha, your wisdom, ministry, and written materials have been life changing. Thank you for the work you both do in the area of blended families. We pray God pours upon you the blessing you have imparted to others.

Clyde and Sue Brewster, for being there for us way back in the most troubling times of our blended family. We will always appreciate you. May God bless all you do.

Our sisters, Priscilla Hilton and Sharon Montagna—you both have always been there for us. You have watched us go through some terrible times, and in those times you will never know how much it meant that we had your love. Thanks.

Our mothers, who are now with the Lord—Joyce and Irene, we honor you today as we thank you for loving our children, helping us as single parents, learning to love our new spouses and new blended family. We miss you both and think of you all the time. You may be gone from being with us in this life, but you are never forgotten.

Our ex-spouses—we want you both to know that we honor you as the other parents to our children. We honor you because we share children with you and you are the other part of those children. We forgive you, as we pray you forgive us, for every past hurt. We love you and want only God's best for each of your lives and the lives of your families.

Our children—we have made mistakes along the way, but we want you to know that the press toward healing, wholeness, and spiritual strength has all been born out of our love for you and our desire to see you have a better future. God will complete all that concerns each one of you (Ps. 138:8). All things work together for good (Rom. 8:28).

Our God—oh, how we thank You for grace. Without You we would have never made it in this blended family. But with You we have learned the power of love, acceptance, and forgiveness. Jesus, You are the greatest gift of all. We love You and pray that the rest of our lives will honor You.

# Introduction

*Happily Ever After—Again?*

**It is ludicrous to believe our
lives won't be touched by blended
families. We need to take their
needs seriously. They are in our
workplaces, our churches, and our
neighborhoods. They are our friends.**

—Hugh Downs, *20/20*

Because you have picked up this book, you or someone you love is
probably in a blended family and trying to figure out how to live
happily ever after again. Most likely there is loss in the backdrop of
the story. In that, we have much in common. We wrote this book
because we know the pain, confusion, frustration, and hopelessness
that can occur in a blended family, and we want to encourage people
toward a commitment to making this new family work—no matter
how hard it seems at times.

Many remember *The Brady Bunch,* the popular television show from the 1970s that detailed the adventures of a happily blended family. She had three little girls, he had three boys, and together they became the Brady Bunch—complete with Alice, the lovable household help. But the Bradys, as much as we enjoyed them on television, were not reality but fiction.

In today's reality version there would be tears, threats, misunderstandings, and a whole lot of messy loose ends—and there would certainly be no budget for an Alice! The Bradys were Hollywood's representation of a newly reconstructed family, a family unit that we have come to call the stepfamily or blended family. We like the term *blended family* because the merging of two families, two histories, two flavors is an ongoing process—a means to an eventual blend. A significant portion of our population is the New American Family, better described as the blended family.

Before becoming the modern-day Brady Bunch, we had high hopes. We hoped that our new family would be the answer to our future and the new lifeline to our happiness. We never stopped to think about the loose ends and fragmented pieces that make up a new family merged by a remarriage. We were two completely different families with different backgrounds, different traditions, different likes and dislikes. We had different rules, different habits, and even different dinner menus! In the blush of a new relationship, many questions went unexplored until we were forced to face them when this new family hit a wall.

You know you're in a blended family when you hit that invisible wall and find yourself related to people you don't know, referring to children that you didn't give birth to as "your" children, and spending energy making financial ends stretch to meet growing obligations. You know you're in a blended family when your time is no longer your own, and you're dancing around calendar dates to make everyone happy. And you know you're in a blended family when you feel like a stranger in your own home, don't know how to play by the rules anymore—because they keep changing—and feel criticized and confused more than appreciated and understood. Sometimes it seems like the reality of being in a stepfamily is being stepped on!

This book is for couples like us who have hit a wall or think they are heading toward one. Or for couples like us who have felt stepped on by the pain of this new life and dare to hope that God is in the serious business of fresh starts, renewed hope, and restored lives.

Our reality has led us to hope in a power bigger than ourselves, because on the flip side of the pain, we have experienced God's grace, love, and forgiveness at work—and over twenty years we have indeed become a blend of two sets of different people committed to trusting God to work His idea of family into our lives. With the mistakes we have made and the hope that God can redeem our mistakes, we are committed to encouraging others in blended families and have worked with many couples over the past several years.

Couples who are trying to navigate their new lives have asked us many questions—lots of *why* and *what if* questions like:

- Why didn't someone tell us it would be this hard?
- What do I do if my kids have a deadbeat dad?
- What if I, as a man, feel like a stranger in my own home?
- Why can't his ex-wife just move on and leave us alone?

- Why can't her ex-husband work together with us to make things better for the children?
- Why is discipline such an issue? Who is supposed to do it now—the "real" parent or the stepparent? The man? Or the woman?
- What if I (the stepmother) can't work with an overcontrolling ex-wife and biological mother?
- Why does the other parent insist on overindulging his or her children?
- What if the rules are different in the other house?
- What if you run out of money after paying all the court-ordered obligations?
- What if the children reject me?
- As a stepparent, what is my role?
- Will we ever truly be a family?

We are not stepfamily experts, but we have the experience of walking the streets of life in blended-family shoes. Ours are a different size and style than yours, but they are the same brand: stepfamily, bonus family, blended family—whatever you want to call it.

C. S. Lewis said, "Think of me as a fellow-patient in the same hospital who, having been admitted a little earlier, could give some advice."[1] This quote describes why we are writing this book. Think of us as people like you, people who have walked the road ahead of you and are going to spend the next several chapters coaching and cheering you on to your place of victory. We are not going to give you quick fixes, but hopefully we will cause you to think, to learn, and most importantly to trust God's redeeming grace as you endure trials that can turn into triumphs.

It is our aim to keep this book both practical and spiritual. We have found that what helped us the most was regaining and keeping a spiritual focus. We will be vulnerable about our misconceptions and mistakes in the hope that you might see yourself in some of our shortcomings and desire change. We pray that this book will give you hope in the power of Jesus Christ, hope in the truth that He wants to live in and through you, making life more abundant than you ever imagined it could be—especially in a blended family!

This new family, often viewed as second best, can be richly blessed. By the grace of God, every blended family can become an opportunity to see His redeeming and restoring love at work. In the twenty years we have been together, we realize just how blessed we are. God has taught us valuable life lessons that can be learned only as we surrender our will to His. Anyone can love those who love them and are related to them. But loving those you aren't related to, people who sometimes reject you, takes us far beyond the Brady Bunch and into the realm of God's love.

Praying God's presence in your blended family!

Ray and Debbie Alsdorf
Livermore, California, 2010

# 1

## Once upon a Dream ...

*When Love and Loss Become Our New Reality*

**White lace and promises,
a kiss for luck and we're on our way.**

The Carpenters

"You have gotta be kidding me!" I was in disbelief after reading the new court papers served to my husband.

I was ranting and pacing as he made his way into the house. Waving the papers in my hand, I let it all out—"How can things go from being so good to being so bad in a matter of weeks? A few weeks ago it was fine for me to be in your daughters' lives, and now, without knowing what hit me, I am suspect at every turn. If I don't put ponytails in their hair, I haven't cared for them, and if I do put them in, they're not the right kind. I send the wrong thing in their school lunches and the wrong drinks for their thirsty little mouths! I can't do anything right! And now—now you're getting served court papers to take away the joint custody you have always had with your girls? How can that be fair? How can she do that? This is not what I signed up for!"

We were only two weeks into our new marriage when reality hit us. Before we had opened every wedding gift, we were opening the gift that would keep on giving—the aftermath of divorce and remarriage.

I suspected that Ray's ex-wife filed the new custody papers because my little boys were now living under Ray's roof and sharing the girls' turf. Add to the equation the fact that another woman was in their life, and you have the recipe for blended-family wars. What once seemed smooth was now turning into a full-force battle. It was hard not to take this slap in our faces personally.

My mind raced through anger, frustration, and guilt. Anger that someone else now seemed to have control over my daily life, my finances, and my husband's future—and frustration that our dream of uniting our two families as one was being dashed right before our eyes.

I went from blushing bride to the wicked stepmother in record speed. The guilt associated with being the one who was apparently the problem was almost more than I could bear. The guilt made no logical sense, because Ray had been divorced several years before meeting me, but if Ray hadn't married me, his custody arrangement would have stayed the same. Watching him fight for his girls broke my heart. This was our new life—not exactly what we had in mind.

## Once a Family—Always a Family

Divorce ends a marriage but not a family. The couple divorces; the children don't, so they remain the constant link between their divorced parents. Remarriages jolt the entire family dynamic, affecting ex-spouses, in-laws, and all the children. In her book *Remarried with Children,* Barbara LeBey addresses the drama:

> The stepparent is usually blamed for any negatives that occur. The wife's family will blame the new husband, his ex-wife, and his children. The husband's family will blame the new wife, her ex-husband, and her children. There's so much blame to go around, it's hard to imagine how anyone can get beyond it. But they can, and will, if they enter the uncharted waters with a loving heart, an open mind, and a willingness to allow for vast differences.[1]

From the beginning of my new life in a blended family, rejection and hurt became part of the routine of my existence. I did not like my new reality. I kept wishing I could turn back the clock to a time when everything seemed to have the promise of happily ever after—a time when everything seemed so perfect.

Most single parents I meet have the dream of meeting another love and living happily ever after. And, according to statistics, most adults do remarry after being widowed or divorced. But the sad fact is that approximately 70 percent of remarriages that involve children are failing. We think it's time to get real about the dream of happily-ever-after-times-two and relinquish it—to the Lord. He can give us what we need to live in a life that is no longer typical, in a family that is not "ordinary," and in a world where our nuclear ideas of family have been blown apart by the reality that our blended families barely resemble a blend!

Our dream wasn't supposed to be filled with anger, hurt feelings, court cases, and costly attorneys. We started out with white lace and promises.

## The Dream of a New Life

It was a beautiful August day—the pale blue sky spread like a blanket with polka dots of white clouds. The morning was picturesque, the perfect day for a wedding—anyone's wedding—but this day was reserved just for us. Everything was perfect.

As the limo made its way to the church, I (Debbie) felt far removed from the bustle of life just down the hill and far removed from the pain of my past. This was my new happy ending—this was the day when I had a second chance at love. It was a day to redeem the dream destroyed by an unwanted divorce.

I (Ray) was about as excited as a man can be. After all, I was about to marry the woman of my dreams. As the limo made its way to drop off my groomsmen and me at the church, all I could think of was how blessed I was to have met this wonderful woman. I was excited about our future together. I was marrying a woman I had fallen madly in love with. Our courtship was something movies are made of. Debbie was the answer to my four-year prayer that God would bless me with a godly wife.

Our invitations read:

*Ray and Debbie invite you to share in their joy*
*when they exchange marriage vows and begin*
*their new life together.*

Our new life together included four children, all within a four-year age range—two in first grade, one in second grade, and the oldest in fourth grade. I (Ray) had the girls and Debbie had the boys. Together we were all going to be the new little family—a real-life Brady Bunch.

The girls looked like little dolls, with curly hair, fancy satin dresses, and shoes right out of a fairy tale. The boys looked like little men with their pint-sized tuxedos, a splash of men's cologne, and spiffed-up hair. After running about the building and doing the silly things kids do, they took their cue from the wedding coordinator and walked down the aisle to the delight of our guests. Once in their places, they waited with the bridesmaids and groomsmen for the wedding to begin. So far, the day was picture perfect.

Most brides are nervous on their wedding day, and I (Debbie) was about as nervous as any bride could be. I stood by the double doors of the church, my heart pounding. As the doors opened and the guests rose, I made my entrance down the center aisle, gazing at my handsome new prince waiting for me at the end of a rose-petaled path. For a moment I felt like Cinderella. My prince's smile melted me, and it was all I could do to keep myself from running toward him and the kids. It was a moment I will never forget—a romantic snapshot etched in my memory. After we said, "I do," we spontaneously gave each other an unrehearsed high five! Our guests laughed.

We were going to make it—Ray and Debbie were starting their new life together.

We would never have believed that just a short time later, in the heat of a custody battle, we would seriously doubt the vows we made on that picture-perfect wedding day.

## The Day We Became the Brady Bunch

At our reception, the new brothers and sisters entertained the guests by singing the Brady Bunch song. We all smiled, chuckled, and applauded. Ray and I felt a flush of parental pride rush through us. Oh, how adorable we all were on that day—Mr. and Mrs. Blend and the little Blends. We assumed that life would continue down this delightful path.

In record speed, the darling rendition of the Brady Bunch song was replaced by the sound of kids fighting, competing, and trying as hard as they could to position themselves in the new family. And we found ourselves in constant squabbles over the territorial rights of our own children. Add to that the ex-spouse dramas, and let's just say our life was quickly becoming more than hard. We were suddenly face-to-face with an enemy we were ill-equipped to fight. Life was about to become more challenging than we ever thought possible.

Instead of a glorious new life, we quickly learned that the Bradys don't exist in the real world—only in a Hollywood studio. I can't recall a television episode where a stepchild or an ex-spouse treated Mr. Brady unfairly. I never saw a show with a court-custody scene featuring Mr. and Mrs. Brady fighting the past to hold on to their future.

There was never mention of strained finances, bad relationships, or past hurts. And Mr. Brady never mentioned a husband-in-law, nor did Mrs. Brady have to deal with the ghost of a wife past, even though both are common in blended families.

## After You Say, "I Do"

We have counseled many couples in blended families, as well as taught blended-family classes at our local church. The thing that gets to us the most is the amount of pain people are in. The pain level in some of our classes is almost palpable.

When doing premarital counseling for those going into a remarriage with children, we share with couples the realities of what to expect after they seal their vows with a kiss. Most couples assure us that things are great, and that though they believe these unfortunate hardships are the experience of some, certainly nothing of the sort will happen to them—they are in love and committed to the Lord. (They all say this and really believe it!)

Sadly, most couples usually call us before they hit the three-month mark. By that time, the realities of life in the blender have begun to rear their ugly heads. What couples can't accept are the same things we found hard to accept—once you say, "I do," things change. Shortly after we tied the knot, everything became real to all involved—and the children, who seemed excited that we were getting married, began their individual struggles to adapt.

It's such a strange contradiction of emotion—on one hand, the new husband and wife are in love and happy to start a life together, but on the other hand, they see the children beginning to show signs of strain and unhappiness. The duality of this family structure can quickly get things off balance.

It became apparent that our new life would be a long, hard

journey of two families trying to merge as one. Our union began to seem more like a collision course than a merge, and emotions were set to boil rather than blend. We had hoped that if we tried hard enough and did it "right," we could overcome any adversity our blended family faced. After all, we were "in love." Maybe you have felt the same.

## We Need More Than Self-Strength

Remember the children's classic *The Little Engine That Could?* The story gives hope that, with enough hard work and optimism, anything can be accomplished. As the little engine chugs along with, "I think I can, I think I can, I think I can...." it makes its way up even the most daunting hill.

Certainly anyone in a blended family can relate to hoping for the future while muttering, "I can do this, I can do this, I can do this...." But once we walk down the aisle, the powers of hell are determined to see us fail. And when that happens, we all need someone bigger and more powerful than ourselves. We need the help and hope that only God, who created us all and understands us all, can give.

How could we have known? Who tells couples these things? We were all wrapped up in planning a wedding, considering what the kids would wear, without ever considering what life would be like after the ceremony. While we were busy budgeting a reception menu, it never crossed our minds that once we took the romantic walk down that aisle, we would quickly be marched back to court. We have talked to countless others who were also blindsided by the change in events once they said, "I do."

## After the Honeymoon—One Couple's Story

Marci and Mike had the perfect life in mind too. They had been married just a few months when problems started to erupt. Actually, they started bubbling earlier, but they took time to come to a full boil. When they married, Mike was forty and had joint custody of his eight-year-old daughter. Marci was thirty-nine with two children—a ten-year-old daughter and a seven-year-old son—and full custody.

Immediately after the honeymoon, Marci's two children became the focal point of jealousy and bitterness for Mike's ex-wife and his only daughter. The ex was insistent that her daughter was constantly being cheated, slighted, and left out. The ex began to tell Mike that his love was now directed only at Marci and her children. Mike argued that it simply was not true, that his only "baby" was everything to him, his heartbeat—but his ex-wife now felt threatened, and she pulled out all the stops to make things difficult.

Naturally, Mom's feelings transferred to Mike's daughter. The girl began to refuse to go over to her dad's new house—because she suddenly didn't like Marci and her two kids.

Mike was devastated. His new life was not supposed to turn out this way. They had planned to be one big happy family. But before long, both Marci and Mike started being territorial and protective of their own children. Both were deadlocked in a competition to protect their turf—the children from their respective previous marriages. Steeped in pride and unwilling to let go, Marci and Mike almost brought their marriage to a devastating halt.

How could this be? They had been so in love, and the children had gotten along perfectly during the courtship. Did some evil switch get flipped? Was this a cruel joke of fate? Would they survive? Why was the real life after the wedding so hard?

## Let's Take a Closer Look

### The Problem

Blending isn't natural and is a challenge for all involved. Mike and Marci found that there was an unanticipated competition based on biological family ties. This competition is normal, but because it was unanticipated it seemed much worse than it really was. Ex-spouses often feel threatened once there is a remarriage and may work very hard to sabotage the children's relationship with both the biological parent and the new stepparent.

### The Path

There would be hurdles to jump and new things to consider, but if Marci and Mike put their heads in the sand (denial) or hardened their hearts (bitterness) toward to each other, or toward anyone in their extended family circle, family devastation would follow.

### The Promise

If they asked for God's help, He would give it. He would answer in spiritual ways that would affect all practical decisions. In Christ, all things are possible—even love in a blended family.

*If my people, who are called by my
name, will humble themselves and
pray and seek my face and turn from
their wicked ways, then I will hear
from heaven ... and will heal their
land. (2 Chron. 7:14)*

### The Plan

Marci and Mike needed to get real, admitting to themselves and each other that this was harder than they thought it was going to be. It was important to quit trying to "play" family; it was time to turn their hearts to God so that a proper foundation for their new family could be established. Without this reality check and the desire for a proper solid foundation, everything else would continue to fall short of what the couple was looking for.

Maybe you can see parts of your dynamics within Mike and Marci's story. Though life didn't end up exactly how they dreamed it would, there were many practical things they could begin doing. Let's use them as a case study and discover how what they could do differently applies to us as well.

- Mike and his daughter needed some alone time to help with the adjustment. Mike was trying to do all things together, involving both his daughter and his stepchildren. His daughter needed to know she had her daddy still and his love always. This alone time would help strengthen their relationship and negate the things her mom was saying about Daddy not caring about her as much as he cared for Marci's kids.

- Both Mike and Marci needed to build alone time with their children into their schedules and not feel guilty about it. In time, after things had blended better, Marci could take Mike's daughter for alone time and vice versa.

- Mike and Marci also needed to look for ways to make peace with his ex-wife. Meetings often don't resolve things, because there is unspoken underlying hurt involved. They needed to start praying for her weekly and to find things that might bless her.

- If Mike's ex-wife was not open to negotiation, they needed to leave her be and continue committing the situation to God and doing what they knew to be right. They needed to refuse to play her game, choose to bless her, and continue to make Mike's daughter feel part of the family in tangible ways.

## What Now?

Because life will not feel normal and will be difficult in the adjustment phase, you will face emotional changes and challenges that you need to keep in check. Find a way to cope with your emotions—get counseling, join a support group, or talk to friends. Make sure you don't confide in your child about all of your feelings. Rather than confiding adult things to your child, make time for your child and continue to build a relationship with him or her. Make sure you keep your word and are on time when you have a parent-child date. Continue living life; maintain your job, friendships, and schedules. Most of all, stay connected to Christ.

The prophet Jeremiah voices God's promise of help and hope:

> *Call to me and I will answer you*
> *and tell you great and unsearchable*
> *things you do not know. (Jer. 33:3)*

When we humble ourselves before God, He begins to do a work in us. But humbling your heart before God is not a quick fix. Blending still takes time.

Author and stepfamily expert Ron Deal likens this new American family to a Crock-Pot rather than a blend. He advises setting the pot on low and letting it simmer toward the blending of flavors and ingredients. In *The Smart Stepfamily* he says,

> Stepfamily integration hardly ever happens as quickly as adults want it to.... Stepfamily researcher James Bray discovered that stepfamilies don't begin to think or act like a family until the end of the second or third year. Furthermore, Patricia Papernow, author of the book *Becoming a Stepfamily,* discovered that it takes the average stepfamily seven years

to integrate sufficiently to experience intimacy and authenticity in step relationships. Fast families can accomplish this in four years, if the children are young and the adults are intentional about bringing their family together. However, slow families, according to Papernow, can take nine or more years. In my experience, very few adults come into their stepfamily believing it will take this long.[2]

There is nothing natural about blending two households together. It's as if you are transported to another country with no way back into your homeland. You are now on new territory with new sights, new customs, and new foods, and you must learn to live according to the new culture—you may even have to learn a whole new language! You are permanently planted in this new land, and you are never going back to the country you previously knew. Dr. Don Partridge calls this new land another universe—like being in outer space. Barbara LeBey's *Remarried with Children* says, "If the joining of two people in marriage is comparable to joining two different cultures, then the joining of two people who have been married, divorced, and have children would be more like merging two different galaxies."[3]

Guess we better get our space suits on and figure out how to walk on the moon! Or at the very least, we need to reidentify who we are now—not who we were, or who we dreamed we'd be, but who we are today.

## Bringing It Home

- Has blending your family turned out to be harder than you anticipated? If so, how?
- Have you asked for God's help, or are you trying to figure life in the blended family out on your own?
- What choice do your actions demonstrate?
- Are you holding on to His promise of healing your family? If so, what specific promises are most important to you?
- Or, as we did at first, are you trying to do this with your own strength, goodwill, kind heart, and fairy-tale hopes of a better tomorrow? If so, how effective has that been so far? Why?
- What are you and your spouse doing to heal your relationships with your former spouses? Remember that God has called us to be peacemakers.

# 2

# Who Are We?

*The Pretty Picture in a Broken Frame*

**There aren't a lot of positives associated with being second. Society says second place, second best— secondhand isn't good enough.**[1]

It was just another typical morning in our new life. Two years after we said, "I do," things still weren't blending. Two separate households were still frantically trying to merge into one, and this new life was stressful and filled with hurt, daily disappointments, and frequent misunderstandings. Some days I (Debbie) just wanted to run away from home.

After dropping off four kids at three schools, I drove my minivan into our driveway and sat staring at the front of our house. *Who lives here? Who are we?* My name was now legally Alsdorf, but my children had a different name. Should our Christmas cards say the Alsdorf family even though half of our family were not really Alsdorfs? I realized that, sadly, we didn't seem like a real family—not in name, not in tradition, not even in pictures. What were we thinking, trying to cram a picture-perfect life into a broken frame?

Slowly, I made my way into the house, poured myself a cup of coffee, and began to cry. At first it was just a few trickling tears, but within minutes it was a steady stream of pent-up emotion releasing like a flood. The intensity of emotion surprised me. I was once again up against the wall, facing disappointment, frustration, and fear of the future. I found myself crying out to God.

*Lord, is this really my life? This isn't what I signed up for!*

Silence.

*Okay, You have all the power in the world. Can You do something— anything—so that we don't fall apart? You know our lives. There is so much pain and awkwardness here—it's all so tangled and confusing. Lord, You can do anything. I think we need a miracle. Please, God, can You help our blended family blend? Oh, Jesus—why is it so hard? I thought this new family was going to be my happily ever after—what happened?*

## Clarity of the Condition

Suddenly I had a moment of clarity. I got a mental picture of a kitchen blender. Through the container's clear glass I could see a variety of family members thrown into the mix. To my surprise, it wasn't just my husband, the four kids, and me—the picture included all the in-laws, ex-laws, ex-spouses, and family pets! Everyone was whirling around like crazy. Grandma's purse was flying out the top, the dog was just barely leaping in; my son's face was smashed against the glass with a look of desperation, while my stepdaughter's eyes were bugged out of her pretty little head as she screamed—*H—E—L—P!*

As this cartoon version of the blended family filled my mind, I began to laugh out loud. We all looked frantic and ridiculous! No wonder it's so hard—all of us whirling in the blades of the blender—each of us just trying to figure out this new family. This blended-family stuff was serious business. A business I was not prepared for. Suddenly the sobering reality of how difficult this new life would be—especially on the children—hit me.

- We were all different—we had different last names, came from different backgrounds, and had different traditions and different ideas about how things should be done.
- We were all hurting and confused—we had holes in our hearts from the losses of our past. We all tried our best to patch the holes, but the emotional baggage was checked in with us as we started this new life.
- We were all trying to smile and make the best of it—confusing as it was, "the show," so to speak, had to go on. We were now playing parts that were not written in our previous life script. Trying to manage this life seemed unreal and surreal.
- We had other family members who were also trying to adjust to the new picture of our family.

In-laws, ex-laws, and ex-spouses were not yet comfortable with welcoming in people they hardly knew—people who seemed to be invading the family turf.

In the whirling of our blender, the smiles were wearing thin. So I sat crying on a beautiful morning—crying over bad attitudes, zillions of misunderstandings, and a life that seemed out of control. Make sure you get that last statement—*out of control!*

I sat still for a while, the dead weight of disappointment consuming me. This was not my path to "happily every after." I didn't want everyone in my blender. I really wanted just the prince. When the reality hits that, behind every white horse carrying princes and princesses to their new remarriage, there is some poop to scoop— there is a mental adjustment to make. This is the beginning of a new family identity. I was now a stepmother, a remarried woman, and part of a blended family. I had a new name and a new life to learn to live in. Learning to adjust was not automatic. Blending takes time.

## What Is Blending?

*Webster's Dictionary* defines blending as "to combine so as to make constituent parts indistinguishable; to mix thoroughly (different varieties or grades) so as to obtain a new mixture; to merge or become merged into one."[2] This definition might work for blending ice cream and fruit to make a milkshake, but it doesn't work with blending people's lives.

Blending doesn't just happen. It is a life we purposely journey into, and the desired results may take years.

The blended family usually falls into one of these formations:[3]

- Both the husband and wife have divorce histories. At least one has young children to nurture. Most often, both have children in the formative years.
- One spouse has been divorced and has children, and the other spouse has not previously been married.
- A previously divorced husband or wife with children has married a partner who has lost a mate to death and is still rearing children.
- The blended family has come about because a spouse became involved in an extramarital affair. The married couple may not have divorced and remarried, but they find themselves in the midst of blended-family issues as a result of the affair.
- A divorced single parent is co-parenting with an ex-spouse. This single parent and his or her children are dealing with the remarriage of the ex-spouse.
- Two single parents are co-parenting and have not yet remarried, but they are living two separate lives and trying to merge the two households for the sake of the children.

What do these people usually have in common?

- A child to care for.
- A remarriage of people who had previously raised their children with another spouse.
- Obligatory involvement of money.
- Another family who has significance in decisions and plans.

- The challenge of loving other people's children.
- A balancing act and a tug-of-war. A parent cannot be expected to quit caring for a child just because of a remarriage.
- A need to learn to live by new rules, much like people living in a new country. The old way will not work in this new family.
- Many difficulties in the new life.

We wished things weren't hard, but they were. Why, oh why, couldn't we be the glorious exception? (Yes, there are some of those, and God bless you if you are lucky enough to be one of them!) We came to realize that there were four things we had to accept in order to thrive in the blended family:

1. Living in the unexpected—this is not a fairy tale.
2. Living with new challenges—there are unexpected problems.
3. Living with new relationships—there are lots of people thrown into the blender.
4. Living with new hope—there is a God who is able to help us. We just needed to make Him the centerpiece of the journey.

## Divorce, Widowhood, and Single Parenting

I (Debbie) hit a wall and was quickly unraveling. I found a counselor to process with and usually left the office tearstained and weeping for hours after each appointment. I went to these appointments alone, because Ray thought everything was fine. While Ray had his Pollyanna glasses on, I was steeped in the unfairness of everything in my new life. Before long I began to doubt that we would make it in this new family. It was too hard. Today it still breaks my heart to see people entering into the harsh land of divorce only to have their bubble burst in the struggles of remarriage with children.

The cover of a current magazine depicts the pain of a recent celebrity divorce. The words "It feels like I failed" are boldly splashed across the newly single mother's face. Under her sad face the caption reads, "Divorce tell-all." Following this statement are bullet points that begin to tell of a future filled with the harsh realities of her new life:

- How to tell the kids
- The fear of being alone
- The difficult transition
- The mad rush to get a lawyer

Divorce is the most common reason people are remarried and in blended families, but it is not the only reason. Some are in a blended family after the death of a loved one. Remarriage after the death of a first spouse brings its own forms of disloyalty and guilt. Remarried widows and widowers often have difficulty sharing activities, rituals, and experiences they used to enjoy with their deceased spouse. Sometimes they won't even talk to the new spouse about the first spouse, because they feel it's disloyal to reveal personal information.[4]

Often children who have lost a parent to death are not willing to allow another parent into their hearts. It seems to the child that doing so will make the beloved parent's death acceptable. Holding on to the grief sometimes is how children hold on to the parent. In these situations, resentment can form rather quickly.

It is heartbreaking when naive children making sand castles and dreaming up big dreams learn far too young that dreams don't always come true. Either Mom or Dad is ripped out of the regular position in the child's life, and everything hurts far more than that child can express. We usually don't see the hurt as hurt but as acting out. And whether or not both Mom and Dad remarry, these children will forever be in a blended family—two households, two family units, two sets of rules, two sets of holidays, two separate parents to pull and tug at their heartstrings.

Also, blended families do not always consist of married couples. A blended family can involve single parents or a combination of a single parent and a remarried ex-spouse. A blended family is any family that merges lives, rules, calendar days, and children with another family.

## Who Are We Now?—One Couple's Story

My friend Annie told me she had reached her limit in her role as a stepmother. She was a beautiful thirty-six-year-old woman who waited years for the right guy. Secure in who she was and where she was going in life, Annie was an attractive catch when Frank met her as a successful forty-two-year-old businessman with two children, ages five and seven. Annie was thrilled beyond belief to meet such a great guy and to be an instant mother. But things didn't turn out as she planned. Always thought of as a nice woman, she now was viewed in every evil way imaginable. Suspicion lurked at every turn.

Though she loved her new husband, nothing could have prepared her for her rejection as a stepmother. Never having had children of her own, she entered this new life with high hopes of a chance to be a mom to two darling but confused little kids. Those hopes were soon shot down—their mother snatched up custody as soon as the ink dried on the new marriage license. No new woman was going to mother her little ones—no way! Mrs. Ex-Spouse did everything in her power not only to keep Annie from the kids but to make her life miserable.

The months that followed were an endless cycle of lawyers, verbal battles, and anything that would facilitate seeing the children. Frank grieved over missing the kids, and Annie felt responsible. She thought if only he hadn't married her, he and his kids would still have regular contact. The whole situation was tragic and unfair.

All Annie wanted was to fit into her new family and make everyone happy. Instead, she took to a new habit of crying in the shower. Daily she cried in this safe place, her back grabbing the tiled wall as she slid down to the puddle of water on the floor. Sitting there in a heap, Annie held her head in her hands and wept. She was safe where the sound of the water covered the sound of her tears. It was just about the only safe place she had left.

Each day her heart got harder and harder as walls of protection encased her, keeping her at arm's length from the joy and love she could experience if she had a new heart with no walls. Her relationship with God seemed to be evaporating, and she said she no longer had any hope for her future.

## Let's Take a Closer Look

### The Problem

Annie had never had children of her own, and the rejection she faced was pulling her under, robbing her of joy. She felt hurt, angry, and powerless—and thus hopeless. Frank, on the other hand, was depressed, missed his kids, and was discouraged because this was not how he thought things would play out. He felt bad for Annie and very angry at his ex-wife, but he felt powerless over her antics—and thus hopeless. He didn't even notice his children's behavior toward Annie.

## The Path

Acceptance of what now is—not what we thought would be—is crucial. Because blended families are a mix of strangers and unrelated people, there will always be hurt and misunderstanding. Annie couldn't control other people, and neither can we. She had to work on her own inner change in the middle of a situation that probably wouldn't change overnight. She had to revert her attention and devotion to God, rather than spinning her wheels trying to make everyone happy. Frank had to look for new ways to parent and be in his children's lives. He also needed to come to a place of acceptance and look for inroads of good. He needed to anchor his hope in Christ, confident that the storms of life would transform suffering into godly character—believing that ultimately healing would come. Hebrews 11:6 reminds us that God rewards those who diligently seek Him.

## The Promise

One principle is important to hold on to—*God is always working and will use the pain to shape us and change us.* Most of us don't want to be changed this way, but pain changes us and can pull us upward rather than downward if we choose to be aware of God in the process.

*In all things God works for the good
of those who love him, who have
been called according to his purpose.
For those God foreknew he also
predestined to be conformed to the
likeness of his Son. (Rom. 8:28–29)*

## The Plan

Annie needed to commit her hurt into the faithful hands of the God who created her. She made a commitment to this new marriage and now needed to hope in God. Frank needed to recognize where his wife was emotionally, caring about her pain and about how his children treated her. Together they had to come to a resolve and a new plan, because the attitudes of his ex-wife and children might not change for a long time, if ever.

## The Need to Move Forward

Moving forward is what we need, but moving forward is easier said than done. I know of one woman who repeatedly drove to her old house, parked in front of it, and cried. She was widowed and then remarried a great guy, but there was "stuff" in the blended family, and she wanted to run away. Instead of running away, she went to her old place of comfort and secretly wished she could have her life back.

When we bleed emotionally, we feel like we have nowhere to turn. We have no idea who we are anymore or who our family is—it often seems easier to just try to manage on our own and begin leaving God out of the equation. After all, nothing feels very spiritual about the whole mess. Can you relate to being a little lost about how to move forward?

## Baby-Step Movement

- Take your wounds and disappointment to God, and ask Him to be the great heart and soul physician for your current need.
- When you come to Him with your life, your cares, and your needs, He places His yoke upon you, and Scripture says that His yoke is easy and His burden is light. Many of our problems lie in trying to do life in our own strength.
- Accept that life in the blended family is hard, and turn to God. Claim His presence with you always. Come to God, advance toward Him daily. Trust that He is your helper, and lean into that truth. Find your confidence in Christ.
- Say with confidence every day, "The Lord is my helper!"

> *"Never will I leave you; never will I forsake you." So we say with confidence, "The Lord is my helper; I will not be afraid. What can man do to me?" (Heb. 13:5–6)*

## Regaining Spiritual Footing

Before marriage, we were seeking God on the decisions we were making. Together we were praying, going to church, and so on. We asked God to forgive us for the sins of our pasts and anything that contributed to our unwanted divorces. We both sincerely wanted

God's will and honestly thought that being together was a redeeming step in that direction.

On one hand, I (Debbie) wanted to be a spiritual woman seeking the will of God—yet on the other hand, once married, I wanted my own way no matter how unspiritual it was. Let me repeat that for emphasis—*I wanted my own way no matter how unspiritual it was!*

I quickly became sick of the unfair environment of my new life and wanted to take revenge. It became my goal to teach others a lesson or at least help them get what they deserved for the pain they were depositing into my little world. I was on the fast track to bitterness—a track that would keep me far from the God whose will I so desperately said I wanted—and far from the biblical truths that I professed.

The imbalance of living only part of my life in dependence on God was making me unstable and depressed. Soon I felt estranged from the Lord, my former source of hope and strength.

After many months of insisting on my own way and insisting on fairness at any cost, I began to realize that what once was an intimate relationship with Christ now seemed long ago and far away. It was in this faraway place that I had a defining moment—one that I will never forget.

I was reminded of the words of Christ in Matthew 11:28, "Come to me, all you who are weary and burdened, and I will give you rest." Those words became a direct call to me personally:

> *Come to me. I can see you are*
> *tired, burdened, and worn out.*
> *I can see your broken heart, your*
> *shattered dreams, and your feelings*

*of worthlessness. I see how you have lost your way, not knowing who you are or if your life has real purpose anymore. I will give you rest from trying to mend your broken heart; rest from trying to be the best wife, mom, and stepmom; rest from the fears of another failed relationship; rest from worry over your children's future; and rest from trying to get yourself together. Yes, I will give you rest.*

I had to admit I was tired. I had to admit that, sadly, as a Christian in the blender I had been plodding down the wrong path. On the outside I looked like any other soccer mom, but on the inside lived a woman bound up in fear, unforgiveness, and bitterness. I had lost myself in plotting revenge for every new situation in this new family. And I was suffocating from past bitterness from a divorce that knocked the spiritual wind right out of me. I hadn't really healed. I was just doing my best to move on and start a new life. But I was building that new life on the wrong foundation—self, unfulfilled dreams, and past hurts. I was just going through the motions of faith.

What is even sadder is that I am not alone. There are many remarried people just like me who are not healed, carrying around baggage, bitterness, the need for their child to choose them over the ex so that the bitter might seem sweeter. The saddest part of this is that it will hurt the children for a very long time—maybe forever.

Before we can move on into a healthy stepfamily, we must first take an inventory of our own heart, our own hurt, and the way we are dealing with our losses. The hurts of our past must be dealt with, and taking shortcuts only prolongs the hurt and blocks the healing we need to move forward. It's important that we look at the past for the sole purpose of moving forward, not allowing ourselves to get stuck there.

## A New Heart for a New Family

There are many things that money can buy—but there is one thing that it can't touch. Though surgeons can give us improved bodies and cut away many diseases, even the most skilled surgeon can't touch the emotionally wounded parts of our hearts. Only God can heal the heart. In fact, He has offered to give us a new model—one that is alive and spiritually healthy. Through the prophet Ezekiel He promises,

> *I will give you a new heart and put a*
> *new spirit in you; I will remove from*
> *you your heart of stone and give you*
> *a heart of flesh. And I will put my*
> *Spirit in you and move you to follow*
> *my decrees. (Ezek. 36:26–27)*

What would a new heart look like to you? If you could take a picture, how would you want to see yourself in this new family? Replay a bad scene and try to imagine it as different—what would that difference look like? Would a new heart and a new attitude make the scene go differently? Is it time to accept God's offer of that new heart?

Think for a moment about the difference between a heart of stone and a heart of flesh. A stone heart is heavy, hard, inflexible, frozen, numb—dead weight. This stony heart is not beating to a proper rhythm—it's off beat, and that funky beat affects everyone's health. A stone heart belongs to someone who is bitter, resentful, unforgiving, and often apathetic about the real needs of other people. A stony heart sees self as the victim and others as the problem. A hard, cold heart—is that God's best? It was never God's plan for us to live with bitter hearts.

A heart of flesh—a new heart— is very different. A heart of flesh is warm, pliable, alive, and beating with a steady cadence. It beats to the rhythm of the music, and in this case, the music is the soul longing to live fully alive and entirely for God.

The music is God's song of love, and the new heart learns to follow along. Hearts of flesh belong to people who have been hurt but have paused to deal with the pain, giving it to God and allowing Him to work in their interior world. Such people learn a new pattern of love, acceptance, forgiveness, and kindness. They become victors, because in Christ they learn they can do all things—including face the disappointments of the blended-family life. A heart of flesh is beautiful; none of us could fully produce it ourselves. This heart is our prayer and desire. It's a heart that understands the gift of grace and forgiveness and the healing power attached to giving and receiving these gifts. It's a heart that understands God's unconditional love.

Given the nature of the blended-family ingredients, it's easy to see why we need a new heart. In *When the Vow Breaks,* Joseph Warren Kniskern says, "What a tragedy when spouses go to war with their children as the ammunition. Instead of putting marital differences aside and fulfilling important roles as parents, expediency and revenge burn and consume everything in their path."[5]

We try to pretend that these new relationships are normal—and that our children won't be affected. But we can't kid ourselves any longer. We need to change, our children need us to change, and God is the only one who can ultimately change us.

## The Way You Were—and the Way You Are Now

Though many things are the same in blended families as they are in intact families, there are many things that are different. Not much seems natural in the blender.

Here are three principles we must learn to accept if we're to discover who we are now and live with hearts of flesh:

1. The new family can't function the way a biological family does.
2. The new family has its own special dynamics and behaviors.
3. Once we adjust to these dynamics, life can become more predictable and positive.

Our American family structure has changed, and now it is full of brokenness: broken marriages, broken children, broken promises, broken rules, broken relationships, broken dreams. So who are we now?

We are imperfect and flawed people broken by life circumstances, in need of a power greater than our own to put all the pieces together again. We are people in need of a focus change—looking upward for a heavenly focus and a heavenly promise for the hope of a better tomorrow.

We are people who need to learn to take responsibility for our stuff and the things that only we can change. If we look to God and take responsibility, we will begin to change. It may take a village to raise a child, but in a blended family it starts with one person who is brave enough to turn a heart toward God and lift the eyes to heaven's resources.

Who are you?

We suggest that if you are anything like the many who have walked this path before you, you are a person readjusting to a new life, needing a new heart, living in a family that desperately needs to learn to live with new hope.

## Bringing It Home

- Who is in your blender container?
- Who are you? Where do you fit in this new picture? Does your frame seem broken?
- Have the blender blades cut you up and hurt the family? How?
- If hope has been delayed, are you suffering with a sad heart? How?
- Do you have hope that God can help you find your way again? Why, or why not?
- Change is a choice. What changes is God asking you to make that would bring healing to your blended family?

# 3

# Learning to Live
# with New Hope

*Going Beyond the Bradys*

**With man this is impossible, but not with
God; all things are possible with God.**

Mark 10:27

We have spent the past two chapters looking at the big-picture problem of the blended family. As we move forward, we will take a closer look at some of the details in the portrait. But first, it's important to take some time to look at a response to all the disappointment, brokenness, and changes. Life circumstances aren't necessarily what take us down; it's how we respond to the circumstances.

How each of us responds springs from what we believe about each circumstance. When we have no hope, we have no optimism for help. Even though this blended-family life has been harder than we anticipated, we have learned how to have a real-life hope in God's ability to help us in the most practical of ways. We want to help you now frame your portrait with eyes of positive hope rather than with negativity and despair.

It didn't take long before we started to feel like a statistic. The boys resented Ray's rules, and the girls had an attitude about me that seemed impossible to shake. We argued more, deflected more, blamed each other more, and pointed our fingers at each other's children more often. Where we started out with patience, frustration had set in.

Nothing seemed to be going our way, and the little bit of family that we had fought to establish was slipping out of our grasp. The girls were in the hands of the courts, and if things continued down the path they were on, they almost certainly would soon be packed and moved out of state.

Gone would be the days of Ray coaching their sports teams, family outings to parks and movies, and our regular routine of Sunday church and dinner. The precious life we had built was evaporating.

The phone rang, and we braced ourselves. As I watched the color drain out of my husband's face, I knew that the call was not good news.

"Are you telling me that as long as I am married to Debbie, I will never have custody of my children?" Silence. "How can this be fair? I am not going to leave my wife. This is ridiculous!"

I could read between the lines. I was the problem, there was no solution, his ex-wife was not going to let go of the battle. She did not want her girls to bond with me and was doing anything and everything to prevent it. She was going to win.

My heart sank, my stomach dropped, and I began gathering my things.

"What are you doing?" Ray asked.

"Well, it's clear that you can't have your girls while you're with me, so I guess I will leave. The boys and I will be fine."

"No, Deb. We can't let this tear us apart. You aren't going anywhere. We'll get through this."

I stayed. We lost the court case. As Ray was openly emotional, the court psychologist put her hand on my shoulder at the end of everything and sympathetically said, "I would not want to be you." I knew what she meant. I was in a no-win situation. I had been hurt for the past few years, but now my husband, the strong one of the bunch, had his heart ripped out right in front of everyone.

*Where are You, God?* we wondered. *Why didn't You answer our prayers?*

But God was working a different kind of win into our lives. We were going to learn how to walk with Him through some really tough times. He was going to teach us about turning the other cheek and praying for others when we felt mistreated. He was about to send us on a new journey of learning how to live in His love, not our own. Ours had been bruised and kicked down. His never changes. And to our surprise, He would show Himself faithful over and over again. Our pain would give us a heart to walk alongside others in theirs.

We realize this doesn't sound romantic, but it is reality. This was tough stuff! One day in the middle of the pain, I had to assess my situation and ask God,

*How can I live like a Christian in the midst of so much misunderstanding, rejection, unfairness, and confusion? Lord, I admit that I don't*

*want to love, don't want to be flexible, don't want to try to see the other's perspective. I am in too much pain for that. So then, how should I live? Can I just say I made a mistake and move on? Show me, Lord, what You want from me in this mess.*

If anyone ever needed huge doses of hope, it would be the person defeated by the challenges of living in this kind of new family structure. What is hope? *Webster's New American Dictionary* defines it as "a wish or desire accompanied by expectation of its fulfillment."[1] Most of us know how to desire something, and unfortunately all of us know what it's like to have our expectations dashed underfoot.

The Bible says, "Hope deferred makes the heart sick" (Prov. 13:12).

Because of this, learning how to have hope—expectation that God is going to come through with help for us—is very important. Otherwise, our children will be raised by parents with sad, sick hearts. With such hearts, what kind of legacy would we be passing to our children?

We have created this acrostic to help you remember what hope means:

H—Heavenly

O—Outlook

P—Produces

E—Endurance

## The Path to Hope

In this book we are speaking of the blended family, but it would be better described as the blending family. The –ing is the most important part to emphasize here. We have learned to find hope in the –ing, because it is ongoing change, ongoing grace, and ongoing movement toward the desired end. There is no such thing as the perfect blended family. But there is such a thing as hoping in God to make your family everything it can be and trusting Him one –ing moment at a time. You will always face emotional hot spots and indescribable times of awkwardness, but most intact families have moments like these too. The key to having hope is viewing things through a different lens.

## Hope Comes with Focus Change

Eternal focus is a key ingredient in changing the outcome of our attitude. The focus must be off other people, outside circumstances, and relentless challenges. The focus must also be off the misfortunes of our pasts. The new cry of the heart is, "Lord, change me!" In this place of surrender, today's hope is found and future hope secured. Though change is hard, it is at the same time full of personal growth and the fulfillment of knowing that through it all, Christ is being formed in you.

How do we get this eternal focus? It's as simple as developing a new habit of looking up. Every time things are hard, look up. Every time you are hurt or mistreated, look up. Every time you are disappointed, look up. Every time you realize things are not quite blending, look up.

Max Lucado says, "It's time to let God's love cover all things in your life. All secrets. All hurts."[2] Each time you look up, remember to hand your care over to the God who can heal and redeem each of life's situations. It's funny how we all want to be happy, but God hasn't called us to happiness—He has called us to a life of holiness. The blended family can change us. For us, it has been a crucible of change. Any situation that forces us to look at our selfishness and confront our attitudes and expectations is a situation that has enormous spiritual value attached to it.

Hope begins when we look up to God with our lives and problems. Hope is sustained as we find encouragement with each opportunity to confront our "self life" through seasons of pain— because it is in these times that God becomes more real to us and we become closer to Him.

> *May the God of hope fill you with all joy and peace as you trust in him, so that you may overflow with hope by the power of the Holy Spirit. (Rom. 15:13)*

## Choosing to Hope

Hope requires a choice on our part. Hope is handed out to us, but we have to choose to receive it, live in it, breathe in its fragrance, and walk in its grace.

The life of Jesus Christ is a message of hope, of mercy, and of light in a dark world. This hope brings encouragement—the knowledge that God is greater than our weaknesses. He is the God of the second, third, and fourth chance—His mercies are new every morning. He never changes—who He is, is a settled fact. We are the ones who must change. We must redirect our attitudes to the good of God, especially when we see the not-so-good side of people. Hope is intentional, something you choose on purpose. In *Hope Pure and*

*Simple*, Max Lucado says, "Don't we have big problems, big worries, big questions? Of course we do. Hence we need a big view of God."[3]

Reflecting on his experience of war, famine, the destruction of his city, and exile, the writer of Lamentations says:

> *I remember my affliction and my*
>   *wandering,*
>     *the bitterness and the gall.*
> *I well remember them,*
>     *and my soul is downcast within*
>       *me.*
> *Yet this I call to mind*
>     *and therefore I have hope:*
> *Because of the LORD's great love we*
>   *are not consumed,*
>     *for his compassions never fail.*
> *They are new every morning;*
>     *great is your faithfulness.*
> *I say to myself, "The LORD is my*
>   *portion;*
>     *therefore I will wait for him."*
> *The LORD is good to those whose*
>   *hope is in him,*
>     *to the one who seeks him.*
>     *(Lam. 3:19–25)*

In this passage, we see some practical principles for getting on with your life and out of the victim mentality:

- Call to mind the truth of God's great love for you, and realize that love is extended from God's heart to your stepchildren, in-laws, and ex-laws.

- Speak the truth to yourself, telling yourself what you really believe and what you know the Lord will do in the final analysis. It's hard today, but God is working out the story of your life, even this moment.

- Ask God to place within your heart His love and value for others, such as the people you may now find difficult: stepchildren, ex-spouses, new relatives. Ask Him for a plan of action in the practical how-to of these relationships. Some may need a cooling-off period, but be praying about a plan of reentry and peace.

## Hope Is Turned Up When We Encourage Others

The quickest path to hopelessness is to keep our eyes downward on people and circumstances or to direct them inward on our personal feelings and pain. Both focus on self. Something happens when we take our eyes off self and look to the needs of others. We begin to get lost in the practice of thinking of others.

When we encourage others, we bring value to them as persons. We help them realize that they are persons with purpose because God Himself created them for His purposes (Col. 1:16). Encouragement brings hope. But encouragement is sadly one ingredient often missing within a blended family, as drawn family lines often make it feel like there are two teams fighting against each other, rather than one family learning to love one another.

> *But encourage one another daily,*
> *as long as it is called Today, so that*
> *none of you may be hardened by sin's*
> *deceitfulness. (Heb. 3:13)*

## Hope Happens When People Are Treated with Compassion and Love

Jesus showed people compassion and forgiveness. People we would consider unforgivable, sinful, and hopeless—He loved them. He hoped the best for them, wanting to lead them into a new life. There may be a person lurking in the backdrop of your blended family who needs this type of hope and love. You might be ready to throw a stone, hoping to bonk them on the head ... but wait—Jesus didn't throw stones but rather offered a new life. Shouldn't we embrace His nature and His example?

Jesus had a style—unconditional love—based on who He was, not who man was. "God is love" (1 John 4:8), and He walked in the style of His nature, no matter what was done or said to Him. The Jesus style is still in style!

> *But Jesus bent down and started to*
> *write on the ground with his finger.*
> *When they kept on questioning him,*
> *he straightened up and said to them,*
> *"If any one of you is without sin, let*

*him be the first to throw a stone at*
*her." (John 8:6–7)*

How does this hope apply to daily life in your new family?

- Your new spouse and children need encouragement.
- Without encouragement, people lose hope and develop sick, hardened hearts.
- You are in this for the long haul. Do the right thing—one day at a time.
- Put your hope in God, as many times a day as necessary. (Debbie used to do it every hour on the hour—as timed by a watch reminder!)

In a blended family, love must be learned. The family usually doesn't blend naturally, and it doesn't do it overnight. In Christ, the unnatural comes to life with His supernatural touch.

## The Hope of Healing Broken Pieces

I (Ray) didn't want to admit just how difficult our new family had become in such a short time. This wasn't what I had signed up for. What had happened to our picture-perfect little family? The kids had been best friends, and Debbie and I had never had a real argument, but now reality was setting in. This blended-family thing was about to teach us some important lessons. God was quickly getting our attention.

Looking back, I see the richness of the journey we had begun together. Giving up was never an option in my mind. What kind of a message would that have sent to our kids? We would be telling them marriage doesn't work and faith couldn't sustain us through the broken times in life. Our kids deserved better. We desired to pass on a godly legacy. To fail was not an option. Before marriage, we had agreed that if divorce was not an option, then the options were to have either a great marriage or a bad marriage. We didn't want to settle for a "barely getting by" marriage.

I thought coming to terms with the brokenness would show a lack of appreciation for the new love and second chance we both had been given. But denial serves us for only so long—in the end it will bite us and keep us at arm's length from who we really want to become, how we really want to live, and how we really want to love.

It's time to admit that our lives are full of brokenness. We have broken relationships, broken expectations, broken promises, and broken dreams. There is only one way we can deal with all this brokenness without becoming bitter, and that is by returning again and again to God's faithful presence in our lives. A lifeline is needed! We need a functional knowledge of God's promise of hope. Jeremiah tells us,

> *"For I know the plans I have for you," declares the LORD, "plans to prosper you and not to harm you, plans to give you hope and a future."* (Jer. 29:11)

Here God promises:
- He plans to prosper us.
- He never intends to harm us.

- He plans to give us hope.
- He has planned for our future.

This single promise given to us by God offers a solid direction for family life. It is time for us as adults to take God's promises seriously. We can and must learn to live a life of trusting Christ. Too many blended families live with hope mingled with despair, and that mixture creates a difficult lifestyle to balance. If we become too focused on the loss instead of the gain, we will always experience feelings of hopelessness. So we have a choice.

Many parents feel they have relinquished the daily role of father or mother with their own children in order to live with and raise their new stepchildren. Their hearts become hardened toward their spouse or their stepchildren as a result of their own loss and pain. But these new family dynamics have nothing to do with our love for our new spouse—and everything to do with the blender. Whether we are divorced or widowed, it is time to pick up the pieces of our lives and move on. It's never easy, but coming out of denial about the facts, embracing God's promise in our brokenness, and then moving forward with hope for the future—these are the path to living well, despite the shattered dreams around us. The good news is, God has given us a blueprint by which to live our lives, and He has good plans—a hope to hold on to—and a future to look forward to. We can find comfort knowing that when the storms of life come, God calls us to trust Him.

Lucy and Charlie Brown put life in a nutshell in a *Peanuts* comic strip some time ago. Lucy said that life is like a deck chair. Some folks place their chair so they can see where they are going. Others place it so they can see where they have been. Still others place it so they can see where they are right now. Charlie Brown's reply: "I can't even get mine unfolded!"

Like Charlie Brown, often we can be left feeling like we can't even begin to get our "blended family" chair unfolded! It is easy to feel like life is leaving you behind. But pick up the pieces from where you are right now and face your future with optimism—there are better days ahead![4]

We can learn to rejoice in the fact that God does have a plan for our lives.

## When All Hope Is Lost—One Couple's Story

Lynn and Charlie were an attractive couple—beautiful in every way, successful to boot. They came into marriage when Lynn was forty, divorced with no children, and Charlie was forty with a ten-year-old daughter from an earlier relationship. Charlie had joint custody of the daughter and lived in the same city as her mother.

After Lynn and Charlie married, they started their own family, and at forty-two, Lynn gave birth to twin boys. When the boys were just three years old, Charlie's daughter, in her teen years, began experimenting with drugs and getting into trouble. Lynn did not want her around—at all.

Naturally, Charlie was not in favor of eliminating his daughter from his life just because she was struggling. So instead, to Lynn's horror, he took full custody of her and moved her in with them, hoping to straighten her out. The trouble was that Charlie was often gone working, and Lynn was left to fix a kid she didn't want to have anything to do with. This was the beginning of the end—or so it seemed.

The daughter hated Lynn, stole money from her purse, purposely ruined her clothes, pinched the little brothers to make them scream—and on and on it went. Lynn took the boys and left. As far as she was concerned, it was over. No way was she going to have that teenage brat in her life.

## Let's Take a Closer Look

### The Problem

Charlie's daughter was causing chaos. Lynn refused to accept that this troubled girl was Charlie's daughter and had just as much right to their roof and to Charlie as their sons did. Charlie was not actively engaged in fathering, so moving her in and expecting the stepmother to "fix" her was not fair and clearly not working.

### The Path

Something had to change. The first change had to be with the adults. They needed to get on the same page. Obviously, the daughter could not be allowed to go on like this, and Charlie should have communicated with his wife and had a game plan before moving her in. Now, he as the father had to take control and find appropriate help and counsel for their situation. Lynn needed to speak up constructively, look for solutions rather than move out, and make a commitment to "for better or worse"—and this was clearly part of the worse.

## The Promise

God promised that if Lynn learned to give out of her need, the same measure she used would be given back to her, double, triple, running over (Luke 6:38). God promised Charlie that whatever time he gave to his daughter, taking responsibility to build relationship with her, would be given back to him by God. No matter how busy Charlie seemed to be, he could not outgive God. His daughter clearly needed intentional giving and involvement from her father at this time in her life.

> [Jesus said,] "Give, and it will be
> given to you. A good measure, pressed
> down, shaken together and running
> over, will be poured into your lap.
> For with the measure you use, it will
> be measured to you." (Luke 6:38)

## The Plan

Lynn had real feelings about the situation, but every decision could not be based on her feelings. Decisions had to be made in the best interest of the daughter and the sons, and boundaries had to be set to protect the boys. A child can't be tossed aside just because she needs help. Lynn had to learn to commit her fears and negative feelings to God, reminding herself that her stepdaughter was valuable to God. Charlie had to protect the entire family, come out of denial, and take care of his daughter's problems. He needed to become actively involved in the parenting of his daughter, remembering that love is spelled T-I-M-E. Both parents had to learn to give to the cause of helping her and protecting the family. Together they needed to mutually craft a parenting plan that was sensitive to the needs of their family.

## Practical Steps for Going Beyond the Bradys

- Attitude change is necessary in these hard spots. Jesus said to learn to *give*.
- Professional help is important—seek the help of a local church, a counseling center, a school resource. Get help; it is out there.
- Protect younger siblings by establishing appropriate family boundaries when there are older children in the family who are in trouble or exhibiting a negative influence.
- Stay positive, love, speak hard truth with love—these are key.
- Recognize that things might not change overnight, but encourage and applaud positive changes as they occur.
- Couples need to recommit to the marriage when things are hard, and this may mean they need to get couple help too.

## Why We Lose Hope

If hope is gained with focus, then it can be lost without it. An inward focus can quickly take us to a place of victim mentality. All of us know people who are always playing the victim role. Life owes them, and they are ready to let anyone know. The victims rarely take responsibility for their circumstances and frequently point the finger at everyone else. Without realizing it, many divorced or widowed people begin to act out of this victim mentality. Their life has been hit by something extremely painful, something that changes things forever. If you are living as a victim, it's time to snap out of it. Reality check—you have been given a second chance! Choose to hope in your future, while trusting God to heal your past.

Though this journey is different from what I (Debbie) imagined, in my heart I hold fast to the promise of God's faithful presence in our lives. What started out as white lace and promises quickly turned into huge hassles and sleepless nights—barely resembling what I thought it would be. It's been one spinning cycle of in-laws, out-laws, and ex-laws—financial stress, emotional stress, parenting stress, and the invasion of another family into my own.

But guess what? This is now my life—I had to learn to accept the truth. This glass blender had become my new reality—my new glass slipper. And like anything processing in the blender, it takes time to get the taste, texture, and blend you are looking for. And, frankly, some ingredients never blend as we hoped they would.

I can still remember that day when I got the mental picture of the blender, when I looked myself in the mirror and said, "Debbie, this is your life; quit feeling sorry for yourself, quit being the victim—get over it!"

I knew I was ill equipped to succeed in this new family, and I was very afraid of failing at another marriage. When I added on extreme fatigue and frustration, it was not a pretty picture. But that emotional morning, with tearstained cheeks and the blender scenario in my head, I said to myself, *This is now my family; this is my life. Something's got to change—and it's probably me!*

We need a lifeline of hope. Not flimsy, gonna-try-harder hope, but solid, unshakable, God-of-the-impossible hope. This kind of hope happens only when we learn to come back to Jesus, daily, for strength, help, and hope. This kind of hope takes place when Jesus is carrying our burdens, making the load lighter than it is without His intervention.

## Bringing It Home

- What is the one thing that makes you feel the most hopeless?
- Do you tend to stay in your feelings, or have you learned to turn those feelings into opportunities to build faith in God's ability to work in your life? If you're stuck in feelings that don't lead to faith, where can you go to seek help? (Don't be embarrassed that you need help with this. Learning to respond in a positive way is not automatic.)

- How can you choose hope and journey into it?
- Do you spend time living with a victim mentality? What fuels that? Who or what might help you break that habit?
- What is one step you can take to begin to turn around your victim mentality, if you have one?
- Why is hope important for you?

# 4

# **These Families Are Different**

*Divided Homes—Conflicting Loyalties*

**I have two sets of parents.**
**I'm lucky, you say.**
**Just try being in my shoes**
**every other Friday.**

Colleen, age 11[1]

I (Debbie) attached a sense of shame to being a Christian in a
blended family. I didn't go about broadcasting the shame; it was just
something I was aware of. Even though this is the most common
type of family in America today, it is still not talked about much in
the church. As a Christian, I thought being in a blended family rep-
resented failure or second-best living. I thought all the intact families
were blessed with God's best, and I was left to get by on second-best

blessing. What a lie from the pit of hell! This shame-based thinking caused me to do some dumb things. One still stands out to me.

It was a normal Sunday morning, four kids scurrying about to get ready for church. Their hair was combed, their clothes clean, and I reminded them of something very important: "Don't tell anyone that we aren't a real family. No one needs to know; it's too confusing. They will just naturally think we are a regular family, so you don't have to tell anyone anything different, okay? Does everyone understand that?"

I'm not sure if I was worried that one of the girls would tell their Sunday school teacher that they hated their stepmom, or if one of my boys would say they missed their dad. Or, worse still, what if they said they didn't like each other! I just didn't want anyone knowing anything about us. We were a normal family! Period.

I still cringe at my personal dysfunction in trying to establish something new in a structure that was very different from anything I had ever known. The truth is, we can plan a beautiful wedding ceremony, buy a rock as big as a boulder for the wedding band, and take off for the most exotic honeymoon imaginable—but if we have not accepted the basic fact that these families are different, it will affect the marriage, the children, the next generation.

## The New Normal

The first thing we need to understand is that blended families aren't oddities to be concealed; tragically, in America they are the new normal. These families are now half of all American families. This means half the population is living with the heartache of division within the household, hassles over financial issues, emotional turmoil over custody issues, and frustration. Even Christians who believe in faith, hope, and love are throwing in the towel because it is just too hard.

The National Institute of Child Health and Human Development's demographic projections reported that after the year 2000 more Americans would be living in stepfamilies than in nuclear family structures.[2] Further,

- Fifty percent of all first marriages end in divorce. Most of those people remarry, but unfortunately, 70 percent of all second marriages end in divorce, and 75 percent of all third marriages end in divorce as well.

- One third of all children under eighteen have already experienced being a stepchild in a two-parent family or will do so before they are eighteen.

- One thousand three hundred new blended families are formed every day.

- Of children under eighteen, 6.8 million live with one biological parent and one stepparent.

- Most divorced fathers are remarried and living with someone else's children, while having their own biological children only for visits.

- Seven out of every ten fathers fade out of their children's lives and will walk away after the relationship fails with the mother.[3]

## Divided Loyalties

Once we digest these troubling statistics, the next thing we need to understand is what tears blended families apart. One of the most important challenges is divided loyalties. What we don't see in *The Brady Bunch* reruns is that in real blended families, divided loyalties flare up as soon as Mr. and Mrs. Blend tie the knot! This division sometimes carries on for years and years. These divided loyalties include the following:[4]

- Parents may feel torn between loyalty to their own children and loyalty to their new partners.
- Parents struggle to balance loyalties between their stepchildren and their biological children.
- Children may feel compelled to take sides between their divorced parents, and they often feel that liking a stepparent is disloyal to the biological parent.
- Children experience divided loyalties among full-siblings, stepsiblings, and half-siblings.
- Spouses may feel a pull of loyalty to their ex-spouse because that person is the mother or father of their natural children.

Jesus has something to say about divided loyalties and the division that happens in family structures: "If a house is divided against itself, that house cannot stand" (Mark 3:25).

Do you want to be a statistic? It's easy; just ignore the loyalty issue and the division under your own roof and keep acting like the children, your new spouse, or the yappy dog is the problem. Are you committed to being undivided—but only in your relationship with your spouse? If the husband and wife are captains of two separate teams, the house will be divided, and eventually it cannot stand. Someone has got to give, and it might be you. It doesn't matter who makes the first move to begin getting things on track. The important thing is that somebody makes that move.

How is a blended-family house divided?

- Juggling two separate sets of rules and expectations.
- Dealing with nonequality in methods of provision or care for the children.
- Not communicating about decisions.
- Approaching your children and your decisions about them as if the stepparent's input has no value.
- Withholding money or resources from your stepchild that you would easily provide your biological child.
- Treating biological children and stepchildren differently.
- Keeping secrets.
- Confiding to your children negative things about your new spouse or their children or relatives.
- Fanning the flame of bitterness between bonds.

How, then, can a blended-family home get unified?

- Spouses establishing agreed-upon rules.
- Preparing and planning for implementation.
- Spouses communicating behind closed doors.
- Establishing budgetary allowances that are equal for all children.
- Committing to treat all children the same. (This is not to be confused with manufactured love. It

is treatment with dignity, rules, and provision all
on the same page.)
- Keeping no secrets—fostering open communication.
- Not bad-mouthing anyone.
- Developing an attitude of love, grace, and forgiveness.
- Developing habits of positive speech and positive talk regarding other people outside the home.

Divided loyalties press in on every side and in every blended-family relationship. But if children are forced to take sides, they will most often boycott the new marriage. In some extreme cases, when children are torn and pressed for loyalty to the other parent, they refuse to speak to the newly remarried parent, often not inviting them to important events, believing that this parent no longer cares about them. It's no wonder that the failure rate of these families is so high. Although the Bible was written long ago, it is relevant to the human condition today—when a household is divided within and without, it will crumble.

## On a Foundation of Loss

Not only do blended families have to contend with divided loyalties, but each is also built on a foundation of loss—either death or divorce. Each family member needs to feel respected, loved, and included, but the time to cultivate love and respect is often hard to find in the hectic schedule of the new blended family. There is a saying that "hurting people hurt people," and the blended family is a collection of hurting people. Many hurts have not been dealt with. The blended family is different in every way. Accept it.

Just take a look at the differences:

| The Biological Family | The Blended Family |
|---|---|
| Related by blood. | Related by marriage. |
| Created by marriage. | Formed out of a loss. |
| Discipline evolves from relationship. | Instant discipline without relationship. |
| Parents' ways are predictable to child. | Everything new; nothing predictable. |
| Couple comes first. | Who comes first? Me or your child? |
| Parents back each other up. | Partners disagree and fight over kids. |
| Child wants to please both parents. | Child wants stepparent vaporized. |
| Ugly fairy tales don't exist. | The stepmonster is alive and well. |
| Competition is healthy. | Competition is for attention and survival. |

The differences boil down to three key things:

1. Hidden hurts paving the way for future injury
2. Divided loyalties
3. Different ways of doing things

## Different Customs

We have talked about hurts and divided loyalties, but now let's touch on the different ways of doing things. These differences range from the simplest things to more important ones. For instance, when I met Ray, he didn't use paper towels—only washable hand towels—and he had never used his brand-new dishwasher. I, on the other hand, always used paper towels and most certainly was planning on using the dishwasher. He was neat; I was messy. He was proper; I was casual. He liked his music soft; I like rock and roll loud.

The funny thing was that the extreme differences didn't show up until we were actually living together on a day-to-day basis. We were very different, so our children were raised accustomed to very different things. How do you take completely different structures and turn those around into a win-win, rather than another loss?

One step is to accept these differences and not respond out of rejection. Rejection is one of the hardest things to face in a blended family. Everyone wants to be liked; no one wants to be rejected. But rejection because of divided loyalties or different ways of doing things is part of the new family portrait. If you are feeling rejected, this is normal. Don't take things personally. Instead, seek to live intentionally and responsibly in these new relationships.

## Dealing with Rejection

Handling rejection is never easy, but here are some facts that we have to come to terms with:

- Our spouse's children will never be our biological children.
- If we are a stepparent, we will always be the stepparent and not the "real" parent.
- Other people now have influence and say over

our lives—people with whom we have never been in relationship before.

- The people who have influence over our lives are people we might not ordinarily be friends with or involved with.
- We don't marry the person; we marry their history, their children, their world.
- We are now living in a different "family country" that has different rules and customs.
- Nothing is fair—we must learn to live in the land of unfair and deal with it.
- Negativity must be avoided at all costs.
- We often feel like strangers in our own homes, in our own skin, and in our own lives.

## Grieving Past Losses

Another helpful thing we can do is to grieve our losses consciously. Every family member has suffered loss, so each one will be grieving privately and sometimes unconsciously. Many people purposely try not to think of their past losses. Instead, they move on to find someone or something new to fill the hole that has been left by a life shattered by death or divorce. It's not the new coupling that is the problem; it's the person's refusal to deal with pain. The pain always comes back later—sometimes much later, but it does come back.

How do couples stop the cycle of revolving-door marriages? How do couples provide a safe place for their children, where blending and loving again is a possibility? How do people come to recognize that they are living with the ghosts of their pasts—comparing today with yesterday?

At one point I (Debbie) realized that I wasn't moving toward God and His love, but in the attempt to protect and preserve myself, I was actually moving further and further from being the person I hoped to be. When I accepted Christ, I had high hopes of learning to walk in His way. But with the entrance of divorce and changed dynamics, everything went out the window. I had to admit that my actions and attitudes were very far from the truth of what God had for me—as His child.

In chapter 2 I mentioned Christ's words in Matthew 11:28: "Come to me, all you who are weary and burdened, and I will give you rest." *To come* simply means "to move toward something." As God gave me the call to *come to Him,* He gave Ray the promise to *hope in Him,* out of Jeremiah 29:11–14,

> *"For I know the plans I have for you," declares the LORD, "plans to prosper you and not to harm you, plans to give you hope and a future. Then you will call upon me and come and pray to me, and I will listen to you. You will seek me and find me when you seek me with all your heart. I will be found by you," declares the LORD, "and I will bring you back from captivity."*

The message is clear—we are to come to God daily, and we are to call upon Him and pray to Him, seeking Him with our whole hearts. We are to trust that God indeed knows the plans He has for us.

Admittedly this was not what we originally wanted to hear. We wanted ten steps to the perfect blend! We wanted to fix the problem. We wanted solutions. Some days we even wanted to kill our exes or each other!

Instead, God gave us Himself and made very real to us the truth that if we had ever needed to walk closely with Jesus, it was now. We were in a war zone, an uncharted territory, and we needed Him to show us how to live. We were about to embark on a crash course of learning how to love—His way.

We pray that you, too, will discover the heartbeat of God, beating with love and longing for you, right there in your very ordinary, messy blended-family life. God has been infusing ordinary people like us with His extraordinary power and presence since the beginning of time.

Whether you have been in a blended-family situation for two months or twenty years, today is the day to come to Jesus with your heart, your hurt, and your future. His plan is to lead you to your own promised land through leaning on Him and believing in His promises. His character is such that He desires not just to fix us but to change us.

## Choosing to Connect

If the Lord is going to build anything of lasting value in our lives, we must first be connected to Him. Our connection with Him fosters love for others. If we want to build something of eternal value in our lives and the lives of our children and grandchildren, we need to remain in Christ, connected daily. Jesus explained,

*Remain in me and I will remain in*
*you. No branch can bear fruit by*
*itself; it must remain in the vine.*
*Neither can you bear fruit unless*
*you remain in me. (John 15:4)*

As we said, much of hope is found in a change of perspective and focus. Prayer helps us in this focus change. We often overlook prayer, but asking in prayer is behind the changes in everything. We cannot dismiss the power of asking God for help, guidance, and grace in our blended families. He is honored, willing to respond, and ultimately glorified through the believer's connection to the power source of His Spirit.

Develop your own personal plan for connection. Be honest about the areas you are struggling with and take time to pray for one another—you might want to start this week.

## Naturally Divided Homes Need an Intentional Plan

Here is our suggested plan for dealing with divided loyalties and conflicting customs:[5]

1. Be proud of the role you are assuming. God has called you to something new.
2. Be realistic. Check all rosy expectations at the door. Don't force relationships. Acknowledge that blending takes time.
3. Love your spouse. Love them by choosing relationship with their children.

4. Be flexible. Take a walk in the other person's shoes.

5. Respect yourself so the children will be free to respect you.

6. Remember that you are not a replacement. You are an original, crafted and equipped by God to meet whatever comes your way.

7. Take time—to adjust, to listen, to pray, to play.

8. Let go of destructive anger.

9. Reach out for help when you need it.

10. Watch for invisible blessings.

The stepfamily requires a different kind of hope, a different kind of focus, and a different kind of love. The good news is, the struggle is stretching us to be a different kind of people. Maybe you feel all stretched out! Hang in here with us—in the next chapter we will address a crucial key to success: understanding the biological bond.

## Bringing It Home

• Is your family divided? If so, how can you get on the same team?

• What are some of the differences in the customs you and your spouse brought to your marriage?

- Where do you see divided loyalties at work in your family?
- How can you, as a couple, keep division at a minimum?
- Have you done the work of grieving your past losses? What next step do you need to take?
- Have you allowed your children the privilege of acknowledging that this family is different and the space to grieve the differences? How can you do that?

# 5

# The Power of the Biological Bond

## *The Key to Understanding*

**Nuclear bonds establish your place
in life and give you your identity.
It's because of the nuclear bond that
a child says, "This is not just a dad,
this is my dad." Nuclear bonds also
identify who is not a family member.[1]**

Our bags were packed, and all of us were headed to a four-day soccer tournament: the San Diego Surf Cup. Hoping for a few days of fun away from home, we headed out of town to the Southern California sun. What could have been a routine family trip for a traditional family turned out to be a pivotal point in our attempt to blend.

The games were going great, the kids were getting along, and we even had some fun downtime with the other adults at the tournament. There were a few little kid squabbles, but nothing too major. So far so good. By the second day it felt like we were a true family.

It all started innocently enough. The problem began with my boys' baseball caps and ended with raised voices, scared children, and me holding back tears and nursing an upset stomach. Though we didn't realize it at the time, this incident marked a classic example of the hurdles that one must jump over to bring two separate families into a new single unit.

My boys were about eight and eleven at the time, and in their first family, the only family that my children knew, my sons were allowed to wear their baseball caps any way and anywhere they wanted. Backward, sideways, forward—no big deal. But my new husband, a police detective, thought backward caps on boys this age were not only a sign of disrespect but also a "look" that made them seem like they wanted trouble. Obviously, my new husband and I had two very different views of how boys should be allowed to wear their baseball caps. Who would have known? We hadn't discussed it before, and we had seemed to be on the same page prior to this incident.

Subjects like this rarely come up during a couple's courtship. Could you imagine dating, and over a nice meal saying, "Hey sweetie, just wondering what you think about boys wearing baseball caps—front, back, or sideways?" It would seem so random and unimportant, wouldn't it? During courtship, your love is all you need. Not so in real life.

No, baseball caps never came up. But the little things like this become bigger than life in a blended family. Two adults, two backgrounds, two previous family rules, and two opinions on life and raising kids. Add to that children who already have had a foundation of rules set before them in the previous family, and now you have the stuff real-life blended-family drama is made of.

Back to San Diego. A few days into the trip, we were starting to show signs of the stress of being crammed together in car and hotel. As the days wore on, we didn't have a spare moment to ourselves and spent the days going from game to game. It was fun but exhausting at the same time. So, we were driving down the road on the last day of our trip, looking for a place to eat, when my new husband got a glimpse of backward caps in the rearview mirror. He told the boys to turn their caps around. Confused, my older son innocently asked, "Why?" And for the record, "Why?" is not what most adults want to hear—especially stepparents who want to establish some authority and respect!

So Stepdaddy explained—"Because we don't wear backward caps in our family." Stop right here. Now you can imagine the confusion.

"But we've always worn our hats this way. Right, Mom? My dad even wears his hat this way sometimes, and he lets us, and my mom lets us...." With that, my new honey gave me a look like, *You better back me up here.* But I was totally lost, wondering what I should do. I just knew that suddenly I was in the hot seat.

It was true that my sons had worn their hats like that before, and I didn't have any problem with it. I couldn't understand what the big deal was. And besides, who said that in this new family "we" wouldn't do that? It had never been discussed, and it was fine with me. Did my opinion not count?

I politely and gingerly said, "Oh yeah, no biggie, the boys have always done that, it's kinda cute!" Oops! Wrong thing to say!

With my "kinda cute" comment, the fur started flying. Words flew in every direction, and they were all directed at me, the mom, who didn't even own a baseball cap! Go figure! My husband got so upset that he pulled over to the side of the road!

Ray wondered how I could allow this. To him it seemed disrespectful and not proper. Just writing about it now makes me laugh, because it really was so small. Hats? Really? The boys weren't being bad; they were sweaty, tired, and had their hats flipped around. So small, so silly, such a stupid molehill to make into a mountain.

But that's just it—the small and stupid things threaten to rip a new stepfamily to shreds. And it all starts with one thing—whose right is it to make the new family rules and to discipline the kids? Weren't these my kids?

## The Biological Bond Is Like Superglue

The most important key to managing life in the blended family is to acknowledge that a blended family is not a traditional family—not a nuclear family—and does not share the biological bonds between parent and child in the first family. Though the blended family has become your new normal, it is not the normal you or your children have known in the past. And it is not the normal you read about in most parenting books. There are biological bonds in blended families, but they are not connected in traditional or neat lines.

Our friend and blended family expert Dr. Don Partridge says, "A first marriage with children is a *simple* family system, with everyone sharing the same biological bond. A blending family is a *complex* family system consisting of biological and nonbiological relationships."[2]

There is no simple way around the new family system. It is complex and confusing. In a stepfamily, a couple may have one of eight or more possible marriage combinations. The life equation becomes extremely complex:

1 woman (+/- 1st husband) + 2 children

+ 1 man (+/- 1st wife) + 1 child (+/- 2nd wife) + 1 child

= 1 very complicated stepfamily

According to research done by Life Innovations in Minneapolis, Minnesota, the average American stepfamily has *40 members*. These include the step-couple themselves, his children, her children and the children they may have together, their former spouses (and *their* new spouses, and *their* children), their siblings, their parents, their in-laws and let's not forget the former in-laws! The family tree quickly becomes a family forest.[3]

## Understanding the Biological Bond

When a woman gives birth to a child, she has a biological bond with that child. This bonded-by-birth relationship is a God-given connection that is part of God's plan. When couples divorce, they leave each other, but the child is still attached biologically to each of the parents. Parents, in their own fits of anger, often fail to remember the power of the biological bond that the child has with the other parent. Your marriage may not have worked, but the children will always need and want both parents in their lives.

There is also a tendency to think that once you marry someone with children, the stepchild will warmly receive you. But the truth is—that child does not have a God-given bond with you. They are bonded to their natural parents. This often makes stepparents feel rejected, and the custodial parent often feels abandoned when their child expresses lots of love for the daddy or mommy who does not live with them.

All is not lost. The situation just has to be handled tenderly and responsibly. Nothing should be done or encouraged that will ultimately damage the bond between your child and their biological parent. And stepparents are wise to not force relationship as if they were now an instant mommy or daddy to the kids who view them as intruders or strangers. Over time, after a relationship is established, you can become love related, even though you are not blood related.

But the child's biological bond to both natural parents is the strongest bond in their life—and that bond is God-given. That is why when we try to consciously or unconsciously replace the other parent, we are actually walking *away* from God's best instead of *into* it.

For an in-depth look at this subject, we highly recommend Dr. Don Partridge's book *Loving Your Stepfamily*. Don is a friend and colaborer in the field of blended families. He is an expert in this field and has much to say that will help you understand nuclear and biological bonding.

In *Loving Your Stepfamily,* he says,

> When a child is born, a powerful lifetime biological
> bond is formed between child and parent. Parents
> may establish close loving relationships with other
> children, but those relationships do not compare
> with the connection parents have with their own
> children. The bond between parents and children
> and the bond between married couples are consid-
> ered to be identical. The Bible makes no distinction
> between the two. The one-flesh bond between a
> couple is considered by the Bible to be the same
> as the one-flesh bond between parents and their
> children.[4]

To simplify this biological bond discussion, let's just make a few
clear points:

- Children have a God-given bond with their biological parents.
- A child's bond to the parent should not be forced
  to change because of divorce, unless for some
  reason the child would be in danger and the situation dictates that the child be protected.
- Children are to be disciplined by the person they
  are biologically bonded to. In the case of the boys
  and the baseball caps, we made a mistake when
  we thought Ray could make rules for my sons
  and enforce them early in the marriage. Until a

bond can be formed with the stepparent, discipline is their bio-parent's responsibility.

- Children need time and attention from the person they are bonded to, so the relationship can continue to grow and the child's loss can be minimized.

- Adults divorce adults, but they do not divorce children. This bond is not to be broken.

- Stepparents must learn to respect and honor the bond that their new spouse has with his or her biological children, allowing the relationship to continue to develop and thrive.

- Stepparents and remarried parents must accept the natural bond that the children have with the noncustodial parent, as this bond is every bit as important as the bond they have with the parents with whom they live.

- Messing with the bond will lead to trouble, because in doing so you are tampering with powerful loyalties (God-given loyalties between parent and child).

## Love Me, Love My Children—One Couple's Story

After just four short years, Paige was distraught over her remarriage and worried that if she didn't do something, she would lose relationship with her children forever. When she married Dan, forty-seven, her own four children ranged in age from ten to thirteen. At forty-five, she was an active mom who had always had physical custody because her ex-husband lived in England, with very little contact with his children. Two of the children were rebels, and two acted like angels. Paige was distraught because Dan couldn't find it in himself to care about the rebelling children. His dislike of the rebels put his wife in the middle by making her constantly choose between loyalty to him and loyalty to them.

Dan had never been married before, and because he had not fathered his own children, he had an unrealistic view of children in the home. He was rigid and had no tolerance for children being children. He was settled into the idea that he would bring a structure that would save the day. But, rather than saving the day, his iron fist almost cost this couple their marriage.

## Let's Take a Closer Look

### The Problem

Paige was a loving, free spirit. Even though she loved her rebelling children, she did not condone their actions. She did everything she knew to do, but she couldn't make their daily choices for them. She was disappointed in them.

But the biggest hurt in her heart was not her children—it was the man she remarried. She had thought he was a loving Christian man, and she was shocked by his refusal to try loving her rebelling children. She felt he was happiest when they were out of the picture, when she was the saddest. She was losing love and respect for a man who claimed to love her and love the Lord. She couldn't believe that he would not try to love her children, who were a part of her.

Dan was at a loss because he had never had his own children. He did not understand the biological bond, and he was governed by his head rather than that bio-bond part of the heart. This disconnect was not his fault, but it was clearly hurting his wife and affecting their marriage.

They had been married for ten years, and they cycled through this problem over and over. Dan had hardened his heart, and though he was a Christian, he treated his wife's two children in a way that many would think is not Christlike. He had tried hardball discipline, but they only drifted further and became bitter because Dan was not their father.

Paige was conflicted. Early in their relationship she had allowed Dan to become the primary disciplinarian. She later acknowledged that she had made a serious mistake in relinquishing what was her responsibility because of a biological bond between her children and her. She also recognized the unfair burden she had placed on Dan. She thought she was doing the right thing by letting him handle the children. Some of the fallout was that they no longer took her seriously.

### The Path

The children told Paige they felt abandoned by her when she turned them over to a man who was not even their father. Healing needed to happen, and it had to start with Dan accepting that his wife had a bond with her children that he did not have and might not even fully understand. It was critical that both Dan and Paige recognize that Paige's responsibility to her children was uniquely different because of the biological bond between them. It was important that Dan have a voice in the discipline of Paige's children, but she should take the lead and become a stronger influence in their lives, taking the responsibility of disciplining her children.

Dan and Paige needed to privately map out a plan behind closed doors, based on mutual agreement. The household rules needed to be clearly defined and discussed. A basic principle to follow in formulating the rules is to make no rule that you are not both willing to enforce.

## The Promise

God desired to change both Paige and Dan. Paige had to commit her heart and hurt to God, and Dan had to commit his inability to love her children to God—asking for His love and strength in their relationship. The way that Dan could show Paige love was by loving her children. The way Paige could show Dan respect was by including him on all decisions behind closed doors and giving him the space he needed to allow God to work in his heart toward her kids.

No one should be pressured to love someone else's children. But that does not excuse the stepparent from their responsibility to nurture and provide. The unstated goal would be that in time a love bond would develop between Dan and the children. If we truly submit our hearts to God, the entire family will benefit.

> *Each one of you also must love his wife*
> *as he loves himself, and the wife must*
> *respect her husband. (Eph. 5:33)*

*The Plan*

Dan and Paige had to come to the realization that when they married and became one, they really became six. Paige had four children that she would forever be bonded to. It was impossible for Paige to separate her heart from her children, and Dan had to accept that, or they would never be able to blend.

The biological bond cannot be understated. It is powerful. Ray and I both understand it with our own kids, but what about when one spouse has never experienced a biological bond with a child? That was the case with Dan. We've come up with a few things to help us through:

- Love me, love my children.
- Not right, not wrong, just different.
- Don't mess with the blood bonds.
- Honor all connections from the biological line.
- Bio-parent is the enforcer for their children.

## I Didn't Know It Would Be This Different!

Couples usually remarry without accepting the vast differences between traditional and stepfamilies. They often end up crashing and burning as a result of not getting real about what they are dealing with. New couples set out to re-create a traditional household. In that setting, the father is the man of the house and the rule setter. The mother and children are expected to respect and follow the father's lead in all things. The father is usually the disciplinarian, except in his absence, when the mother upholds the family rules and values.

This model might work in a traditional home where both mother and father have the biological connection to the child. The child is not confused, and it is how God intended. This model is the biblical model we may be comfortable with—and this is where Christians in stepfamilies get confused and tripped up. In a remarriage with children, things are different because of the blending of biological and nonbiological bonds. Trying to enforce the traditional model with nonbiological children hinders successful blending for all involved.

One husband we know said that he felt he was married to his wife and that she was married to her children. He was joking, but his sentiment was serious. He had no idea that his new wife would sometimes choose the children over him. He underestimated the biological bond that had been well-established for years. This bond naturally causes people to love and protect one another. It is a one-flesh bond.

This feels foreign to us as we think of marriage and family, because most of us are familiar with the original model of the husband and wife leaving all behind and cleaving to each other only. This was God's design for the family. The family was to begin with their physical and emotional separation from their families of origin—they leave and cleave to each other, thus forming a new family foundation. The marriage relationship is established before children. God designed marriage to be a sacred one-flesh relationship.

Scripture even speaks of the importance of marital bonding in the first year, which we have called the honeymoon period. Moses wrote, "If a man has recently married, he must not be sent to war or have any other duty laid on him. For one year he is to be free to stay at home and bring happiness to the wife he has married" (Deut. 24:5).

Blended marriages don't enjoy this same honeymoon period. And when children are involved, a parent does not emotionally detach from a child in order to begin a new relationship. Parent-child relationships are bonded biologically, and they have history that doesn't erase and should not be ignored. The parent-child relationship is often the strongest in the new family, with the new marriage being the weakest. This creates confusion from day one.

This feels unnatural, and it is. But there is no going back once you have children in your life. They must be a priority, and you cannot leave them for another. Well, you can—many do—but it is not God's best for you or for them.

We have looked at the foundational differences and problems in blended families—our need for hope, and our need for a strength greater than our own. Now we acknowledge the bio-bond and how it trumps all else, must be tended to, and cannot be ignored. As we move on we will begin to look at the many different details of blended-family living, beginning with the new family structure and the most common of all questions, "Who is the head of the blended-family house? And who is in charge of the kids?"

## Bringing It Home

- If you are a biological parent yourself, stop and think of the powerful bond you have with your child. Do you resent when someone tries to change or rearrange that bond? How do you show that?

- How does it affect you when your bio-child is treated unfairly or too harshly? What do you do?
- Do you feel the same way when your stepchild is treated just as harshly?
- How can you as a stepparent be more understanding of the biological bond?
- Do you ever assume your way is the right way? How is that working for you?
- How would it affect you if your spouse learned to unconditionally love your child?

# 6

# The New Home Front

*Discipline and Family Structure*

**Where a stepfamily is loving and
nurturing, and where the children are able
to continue good relationships with their
natural parents, they will thrive almost
as well as children from intact families.[1]**

Imagine walking into someone else's life and being told, "This is
now *your* life." Pretty weird, huh? Yet that's what it's like for families
thrown together in the blender. There are so many uncomfortable
variances. Who gets to be right? It is so confusing.

Recently a woman told me that she was stressed every time she
walked through the door of their home. Why? Because she had to
make sure that her three children from a previous marriage always

minded their p's and q's. "It's like walking on eggshells, and I feel like I'm holding my breath! I just want to exhale," she said.

This is the sentiment I hear over and over. Men say things like, *I feel like I am just a meal ticket, no one really cares about me or what I want—I am a stranger in my own home.* Men complain of not being respected, while women complain that they are a bridge between two countries—always blamed and walked on! Both parties are walking on eggshells. The children are caught in the fray. All involved are uncomfortable in their own home and in their own skin.

Ray had some very solid ideas about how boys should be raised. Most of them I supported and agreed with. But some were hard to swallow. There seemed to be a parental tug-of-war and confusion in our roles. I have found this to be the case for many couples who bring children into a relationship. We aren't willing to just turn our children over to someone who has no significant history with them.

For example, take a Christian woman with three children who remarries and has physical custody of her children. They see their father on alternate weekends and on school breaks. They are used to living according to their mother's standards, because she is their primary caregiver. But now these three children are expected to answer to a stranger they hardly even know—their stepfather—and are moved into a new house they aren't comfortable in.

Mom is not aware of the loss her children are facing. She is in love, and her head and heart are in the clouds. At first she easily relinquishes all rights to her new man in the name of love. But soon, confusion sets in for the children as they watch their mother's attention and loyalty shifting to a man who has a whole new way of looking at life. In the children's eyes, this new man is simply an intruder stealing Mom's attention. He took their mom, set up new rules, and is not their dad. This is a recipe for trouble. They decide he is the enemy.

Mom becomes the traitor as quickly as the new stepdad becomes the enemy, and the children are left confused. They might ask to live with the other parent or begin rebelling and acting out in ways that create even more problems. It's time to get biologically balanced if we are going to see stability for future generations of children living in these families.

As we said in the last chapter, children are biologically connected to their parent, not to their stepparent. To try to come between a parent and child is like trying to peel apart layers of something that has been bound with superglue. Not only is it hard, but usually the bond is so strong that it borders on impossible. So rather than trying to mess with God's biologically created bond, we need to learn to work with it—together. As parents in a blended family, we need to acknowledge the built-in complexities that exist. To deny they exist is a slippery slope. A recipe for failure.

Again, it bears repeating that each blended family has a different set of connections. A connection between biological children and their parents does not change; it is forever. Even in the case of an absentee or deceased parent, the connection remains. Once a parent, always a parent—there is a God-given biological bond. That bond is not broken by remarriage, and that bond does not belong to the new spouse or stepparent. Seems simple to understand, right? Well, it's not that simple in practice.

Here's the catch: Consider a blended family with a mother, a stepfather, and children. Because of the biological bond, it's the mother who has the primary role of parent to the children. She is the one biological bond in the mix. It is her responsibility to uphold the family rules and standards, *until* a bond can begin to form between the children and their new stepfather. And even after that bond of affection is formed, it is still best for the biological parent to parent her children.

Is this going against the biblical standard of the man being the head of the house? No, not at all. The husband is still the head. The new wife has made that agreement, and if she desires to live biblically, she will uphold and respect his position in the family—as the head. She will submit to him as her head and covering, and he will love her, which will mean accepting her children and her bond to them.

As the rules of the new family are made, it becomes the biological parent's primary responsibility to enforce them because of the natural bond between her and her children. It is critical that decisions affecting the children be made as a team. The nonbiological parent must have a voice in the making of rules, but the primary enforcer of the rules has to be the biological parent. As times goes by and as healthy bonds begin to grow between the children and the stepparent, the responsibility of the enforcement of the family rules can be shared more equally.

The key is building a relationship of caring and trust with all involved. As a general rule, we encourage parents to form a united front. We also understand that this goal is not always immediately achievable. But when we establish and enforce family rules, it is crucial that we do not allow a power struggle to ensue, but that we labor to resolve issues, working to find a solution that works for all involved.

## The Blended-Family Map

It took some time, but we ended up seeing something that has been life-changing and family-saving for our new marriage. And here it is: We each had different views on things—and neither of us is right or wrong; we are just different people. Pretty simple, right? Each of us has a different way to work around a problem or a different mapped-out way to do things. Then why do we insist on thinking that something different from how we have always done it is wrong? This often becomes the root of bitter power struggles. I am right—you are wrong. This has to be turned around so that the couple can turn the corner and get to the desired destination—peace in the blender!

In a first marriage, this difference gets absorbed over time. Children enter the family picture that the couple has already established with their way of doing life. Usually by the time a family is started, the couple has some similar ways of doing things. But even then, there will always be differences, because they are different people.

In intact families when children come along, the children aren't confused; they have one mom and one dad who have always been there. Conflict will still arise, but for the most part, the power struggles are far less intense than in the blended family.

## Submission in the Blended Family

Most women run from the word *submission*, and many Christian men use it as a weapon, because neither fully understands God's plan. Submission is not a weapon or anything to be feared. Submission is not being a doormat. It is placing yourself in position to be empowered to be all you were meant to be.

Anything that God has laid out for us is for our good, and if we embrace it, it leads us into a larger place of freedom. But in our human nature, we want our own way, insist that our way is right, and want to be treated fairly. So in the blended family, it is important to look at the word *submission*. Paul tells us:

> *Submit to one another out of reverence*
> *for Christ. (Eph. 5:21)*

This is the foundation of *all* relationships. The word *submit* means "to be subject to," or "to be under the authority of another." Basically it means to put others first.

Submission has gotten a bad rap. It isn't just for marriages—it's the caring, strength, kindness, and humility that can make any relationship stronger. That's why Paul tells us to submit to *one another*. It means to think of someone else's needs, not only your own. And it means placing yourself under the authority of Christ as your Head: Submit *out of reverence for Christ*.

Honestly, with Christ as our guide, the main thing coming out of us would not be anger, threats, and pride—rather, it would be the fruit of His Holy Spirit: love, joy, peace, patience, goodness, kindness, faithfulness, gentleness, self-control (Gal. 5:22–23).

## The Husband as Head of the House

If a man is to be the head of the home and the example of leadership to his family, he must learn to think of the others' needs and not just bend things to his own ideal. In a biological family, he has history and has authority over all involved. He also has a natural bio-bond of love, a one-flesh bond with both wife and children. But in a blended family, there is no history, and he does not actually have even legal authority over the stepchildren. There is also no bio-love bond, and love takes time to cultivate in the blended family. It often takes years. So in a blended family, who is the head, and who is in charge of the kids?

Let's look at how the family structure in Ephesians 5:21—6:4 builds a foundation for a family, blended or not:

- Wives are to be subject to their husbands.
- Husbands are to love their wives sacrificially.
- Children are to obey their parents.
- Children are to honor their mother and father.
- Fathers are to treat their children fairly and not exasperate them.

Biblically, it's a no-brainer when it comes to a first family—one husband and one wife, one father and one mother—all biologically intact. This is God's plan. But what happens when this intact family has been splintered or disrupted by death or divorce?

Parents and children scramble to find their places when lives are splintered. The power struggle has to stop if the blended family is ever going to blend and become a new, strong unit. In a remarriage, usually two heads of households merge to become one. So who gets to be the new head?

Let's apply the family structure described in Ephesians. The husband is still to be the head over the wife. But who is to be the head over *her* children? The passage states that the children are to obey their parents. But in a blended family the children live with only one biological parent, either the father or the mother. *They are to obey that biological parent.* If this parent is a mother, this plan may feel confusing to the new husband, who wants to be the head of things and may struggle with control issues over the new kids.

How then can a woman be subject to her husband in all things, if she is acting as head over the children? The woman is to submit to her husband as his wife. But this new wife has children, over whom *she* is the head. The new husband is the covering for the entire household, but the biological parent must continue raising her children, under his covering.

Can the stepparent have a say in how she raises the children? Of course! They are all living together, so daily living arrangements must be agreed upon. And it will then be the mother's responsibility to be the enforcer of her husband's wishes on mutually agreed family protocol. When the couple can't agree, the mother will have to make the hard call. If she doesn't keep her position as the children's parent, they will be lost and insecure. They will feel like they have been abandoned.

## Blended-Family Model

This, then, is the model we believe is most biblical for blended families:

- Wives are to be subject to their husbands. The new husband is the head over the wife, and she is to yield her life toward him.
- Husbands are to love their wives sacrificially. In these families, this involves loving her children, who are not natural to love—so this is truly sacrificial love.

- Children are to obey their parents. *Parent* here means biological parent. The stepparent is not the parent. The biological parent is the one who must direct his or her own children.

- Children are to honor their mother and father. Children need to be encouraged to maintain relationships with both biological parents, even one who may not be living near or with them. Children are to be taught to respect the new stepparent—to respect, not to view as a replacement of the biological parent.

- Fathers are to treat their children fairly and not exasperate them. Fathers, this is no time to fade out of your children's life! They need you. Be loving, gentle, and caring about their hurts, their hearts, and their practical lives. Stepfathers are to treat their new stepchildren fairly.

- Likewise, if a woman is a stepmother, she needs to learn to love her husband's children in a way that will require her to think of others above herself.

This mutual submission, this thinking of others above oneself, is key to the success of the blended family. It is not standing entrenched in our own rights or our own practices, traditions, or opinions. Instead, it is being open to what can merge to become a new tradition or practice in the new family. Submission is gentle. Submission is not weakness; it is living with strength but not aggression at the core.

And this one simple word, applied to all family members, will make the biggest difference imaginable. It is a walk of self-denial, which we are not very good at, and humility, which most of us could use more of.

## A Test Case

Recently a friend of ours said that her new husband does not approve of her going into her children's bedroom at night to read and pray with them. He is a very nice man and a Christian man who values prayer. What's the problem? He feels that the children are manipulating their mother during this hour, that they just want to extend their bedtime. The mother understands, but she has always read to them and prayed with them. For a few weeks she stopped but found herself feeling resentful, and her children felt they had done something wrong.

Everyone in the household except the stepdad was confused. Finally, the mother spoke up and told her husband that because reading and praying were their family routine before he arrived, she would continue with it. She loved it, the children looked forward to it, and she asked him to accept it. He was insulted at first, believing that she was naive about her children's plot. But in time he realized it wasn't that big a deal, and he began to see how he was the one who would have to make the biggest compromises, because he was now living with a family structure that already had a set way of functioning.

It will go much more smoothly if the biological parent handles his or her own children initially—and this initial period could be a few years. This gives the children opportunity to develop a bond with the stepparent, and in time it will become natural to be subject to the stepparent in the same way one would be to the biological parent. That is, if the stepparent doesn't blow that opportunity by being too demanding in the beginning. Give the children a break. Let them adjust. Insist on obedience to their biological parent. And decide on the rules or goals of the family in private, as two married adults, then allow the biological parent the position of enforcing the rules that both of you have agreed to.

## The Wife in the Blended Family

How is the wife to live biblically and in a way that balances real life in the blended family?

- Communicate with your spouse, out of respect. Make talking about differences safe. Take turns talking and listening to his point of view. In many cases he is more objective than you can be.
- Remember that your ideas are not always right. And your spouse's are not always wrong. Not right or wrong—just different.
- Acknowledge that you cannot always have your way.
- Put aside your own interests, when necessary, to join your life with his.
- Respect the position in which God has placed your husband as your covering.
- Respect the position of biological parent, and take the responsibility attached to that seriously, while learning to balance respect for your new husband.
- Respect his children, and honor them by learning to love children who are not your own. Love begins with familiarity and friendship, and these take time. Give them time.

- Respect the commandment about children loving their other natural parent, and help them keep that biological bond strong and secure.
- Remember that your spouse and his children had a life before you, and don't block or interfere with connection and respect of any of those bonds, where they are appropriate.
- Resist the urge to compete with the children. A power struggle with the children is a lose-lose for all. Consider the children—they are people who have been forced into this new family. They didn't choose this.

## The Husband in the Blended Family

How is the husband to love his new wife biblically and in a way that balances real life in the blended family?

- Be willing to sacrifice everything for her, which includes learning to love her children.
- Make her well-being of primary importance.
- Be patient with her as she learns to balance children and a new husband.
- Allow her the freedom to be the mother God made her to be without worrying about your getting jealous or demanding of her time and attention.
- To love a mother, you must love her children. Period.
- Be honest about the things that are important

to you, and be willing to strike an agreed-upon compromise when necessary.

- Help her with the children in the practical areas, while giving her the responsibility of enforcing the agreed-upon rules.
- Take your position as the man and head of the household seriously, and use that position as an opportunity to be the most loving person in the family.
- Enforce the agreed-upon rules with your own natural children when they are with you.
- Don't expect your wife to be the primary caregiver for your children. You did not marry a nanny; you took vows to make her your wife.
- Husbands, love your wife as Christ loved the church. This is laying down yourself, a sacrificial type of love. If you did not learn this the first time around, you have been given a second chance.

If Ray and I had talked about baseball caps before that episode in the car, we might have come to an understanding on that. Or we might have agreed to disagree and allowed the boys to continue wearing the hats in the manner they always had been used to. Communication is the biggest issue. Once something has been communicated, then submission of the wife to the husband, love of the husband to his wife, and children's obedience to the parents all begins to make more sense. The goal in a blended family, or any family, is to be in healthy submission to one another. Putting the others first. This is taught by modeling, and this modeling is tricky in the blended family.

## Discipline in the Blended Family

Most stepfamily experts agree that, at least initially, the biological parent should discipline his or her own children. Children are already confused and respond to their own parent much more readily than a new stepparent. The relationship with a biological parent has existed for a long time. There is history and a readiness toward forgiveness. While children may resent a stepparent applying consequences, they will expect a biological parent to rein them in and set boundaries.

This doesn't mean the stepparent has no say or is invisible. The trick is in how the couple handles discipline in front of the children and the details that go on behind the scenes.

According to the *Webster's New Collegiate Dictionary,* discipline is:

1. instruction
2. a subject that is taught
3. training that corrects, molds, or perfects
4. orderly or prescribed conduct or pattern of behavior[2]

Discipline is not just punishment, but establishing standards of behavior and setting family boundaries and limits. The new couple should set these standards behind closed doors, and then the biological parent should initially enforce the agreed-upon rules.

What happens when children act out when the biological parent is not home? The stepparent then reminds the children of the rules, asking them to comply with the house rules. If they don't comply, then it's appropriate to calmly set some immediate consequence that does not go into a place of anger or yelling or in any way touching the child. The stepparent communicates with the biological parent what has happened—and here is the key to success—*the biological parent trusts what his or her spouse says happened* and then enforces rules with the children. This must be consistent for the house to run smoothly. In this way, the child knows that when Mom or Dad is not present, the stepparent has authority to take care of things and will communicate with the mom or dad. In essence, the biological parent lends the right to discipline the children to the stepparent.

But what if you don't trust that your new spouse, the stepparent, has your child's best interests in mind? This certainly can be an issue in blended families. We would all like to think that we would love someone else's child in a God-honoring way, but the truth is, it isn't easy to live with a child who is not your own, has different ways of doing things than you do, and has a negative bent toward you just because you are not their "real" parent.

## Do Stepparents Become Prisoners in Their Own Homes?

There is something very lonely about being a stepparent, and that hurt can form a wall between a stepparent and the child he or she originally thought it would be a "piece of cake" to love.

Don and Jenetha Partridge offer a number of possible solutions:[3]

1. Don't sweat the small stuff. Stepparents have to let a lot of things go.
2. Consult a third party. Be sure the third-party individual is part of a good, working blending family. First-marriage adults usually don't get it.
3. If the parent is unwilling or incapable of managing the child and you are powerless to help, a very

effective solution is to allow the child to experience failure. This is a long-term solution but is
very, very effective. Continual suffering usually
brings maturity.

4. If you can't control your stepchildren, you can
   still control your own. Don't hesitate to set up
   separate rules for your own children.

5. If you feel unsafe living with an unmanageable
   teenager or adult child, take your children and
   leave the household, living elsewhere until the
   child is older and independent of the family.
   You are separating from the child, not your
   spouse. For your peace of mind, you need to
   live in a separate place.

## Coming Up with a Plan

It is important to have a plan as a couple. You can't implement
discipline without household limits, expectations, and plans. This
requires that the couple decide, albeit idealistically at first, what the
family mission statement will be. The household plan must then line
up with that statement and be agreed upon by each adult. The plan
will be tweaked over the years as you continue to blend and adjust.

We came up with a mission statement of wanting to raise our children in a Christian environment, with biblical modeling. We wanted
our children to be all God had planned them to be. That required us to:

- Give them boundaries to help them grow.
- Give them understanding to help them learn.
- Give them a voice to help them learn their value.

- Give them love to help them be secure.
- Give them wings when they grew up and were ready to fly on their own.
- Give them a life model based on how we lived.

Rules and boundaries are not about being mean or authoritarian—they are a way to give to your children what they need as children. Find freedom in that. Discipline is an act of love, an opportunity for teaching.

> *"The Lord disciplines those he loves, and he punishes everyone he accepts as a son."* ... *God disciplines us for our good.... No discipline seems pleasant at the time, but painful. Later on, however, it produces a harvest of righteousness and peace.* *(Heb. 12:6, 10–11)*

In following God's example to us, we are to set limits for our children and train them in what would be beneficial for them. They will not like limits or rules—but that's okay. Discipline seems painful at the time, right?

Here are some things that need structure and planning:

- Bedtime
- Household expectations
- Household responsibilities and chores
- School expectations and grades
- Movie and media ground rules

- Curfews
- Dating ages
- Phone usage
- Allowances
- Employment
- Modesty/privacy
- Budgets for clothing
- Friend invitations (home and away)
- Mealtimes
- Menus/food
- Extended family interactions
- Gifts

These are just some suggestions, and now we challenge you to think about these as you create your own list.

## Let's Take a Closer Look

### The Problem

Does the fact that discipline and family structure are different throw you a curveball? It does for most people, and it creates a problem. Remember that the biological parent is the one mandated by God to care for his or her children. The bond is between parent and child, and though a stepparent can step into the child's life, that person is not the parent. What does this bring up in your couple relationship that needs to be addressed?

## The Path

Come up with a plan that works for you as a couple. Take some time to be alone and talk about this chapter. Identify your differences and then come to a compromise that will work for both of you. The stepparent then needs to relinquish control, while the biological parent needs to make a commitment to respecting the wishes of the new spouse and take his or her differences and wishes to heart. When appropriate, both need to embrace a spirit of compromise.

## The Promise

God promises to make our paths straight when we trust in Him and look to Him for help. In these families, that is like saying He will work out the blend.

> *Trust in the LORD with all your*
> *heart*
>> *and lean not on your own*
>> *understanding;*
> *in all your ways acknowledge him,*
>> *and he will make your paths*
>> *straight.*
> *Do not be wise in your own eyes.*
> *(Prov. 3:5–7)*

## The Plan

Admit that your own understanding and what seems like wisdom to you may not be the best thing. Make a personal decision to choose to come to God with everything as the need arises. Learn to ask, "Lord, I don't know what to do, so my eyes are now on You. How should I live and respond in this situation?"

We have covered many points that can make a difference, if we pay attention. Repetition can make ideas clearer and this helps us hold on to hope, so let's recap what we have been building on up to this point:

- Blended families are hard and represent some loss. We are all cut up in the blades along the way. Baby steps forward are reasonable. We need to put our hope in God and frame our perspective more positively. How we frame life will determine how we live it out.

- These homes are often divided in loyalties—or loyal TIES. Acceptance of what *is* is important. The biological bond is the key ingredient that must be preserved for security and stability.

- Each spouse must accept the biological bond. Submission and humility are the pathway to finding balance. The bio-parent is the enforcer initially—until love bonds are later formed. We need a family mission statement and clear family rules.

- You are responsible only for what happens under your roof. You are ultimately responsible for your heart of submission to God.

## Bringing It Home

- Have you and your spouse talked about a family mission statement? If not, why not?
- If a mission statement declares what you hope your outcome will be, what will your mission statement say?
- What could be changed to make your family structure more balanced?
- Do you need to sit down and create a list of things that you want to have clear expectations on? If so, when can you do that?
- Have you decided what appropriate discipline or punishment will be when the child does not meet the expectations? When can you take time to do that with your spouse?
- Have you given thought to what it would mean for you personally to submit to God? When can you determine that?

# 7

# **Attention to Details**

*Holidays, Money, Custody,
and Other Nuts and Bolts*

**Parenting in stepfamilies is a two,
three, or four-person dance.**

Ron Deal

As a single mother, I had the responsibility of handling my children's calendar—scheduling times for fun as well as enough time for work and responsibilities. I also had the responsibility of working out visitation with their father, handling financial obligations with the little money I had, and figuring out how to make ends meet. I carried a calendar, kept to the schedule, and had a plan. Humanly speaking, I was in control.

Then, just when I thought I was getting a structure and a routine in place, I remarried. Now someone else had control over my days, my plans, my calendar. The problem was, this someone wasn't my new husband as much as it was his ex-wife and the other household. Maybe you can relate.

I was distressed over needing to have her approve dates and plans, and I'm sure she didn't like to have me looking over her shoulder either. Truth is, in a blended family your schedule is no longer just your own business. It now involves other people—often people you hardly even know.

A discouraged stepmom told us,

> My young boys had been with babysitters and in kids' camp almost the entire summer. It was obvious they missed me. After my remarriage every fun thing was planned for the times my new husband's kids were with us. The boys and I rarely did anything fun together anymore. Trouble was brewing, because the boys knew that the other kids had plenty of fun with their own mom when away from them. It was becoming apparent that the imbalance was hurting my kids. So, I launched out for the very first time since remarriage by taking my boys, all by themselves, to Marine World. This was a big step for me, because it did not include the stepkids, who were at their mother's house across town that week.

> Knowing that my kids needed me and my individual attention, I took the risk of rocking the boat and maybe even capsizing it for awhile. The day was spectacular. It was worth every penny and every fear

that it would stir the pot and cause me trouble later. And, as expected, the boat crashed! My husband's ex-wife was very angry that I didn't include her kids, and got the kids to be angry and hurt too. Pretty soon even my own husband was questioning why I went without his children. Was I confused? You bet! Was it hard to be criticized for spending time with my own children? Yes! Would I do it again? Of course! Sadly, that one-time outing with my own children cost me—I paid for it for many months. Any ground I had gained with my stepchildren was lost over one day at Marine World![1]

We related to this story and many others like it that we have heard. In the early years we too thought everything had to be done together, and we tried very hard to make our family feel normal. But as we've said in past chapters, the quest for normalcy just leads to further frustration and disappointment. A new normal has to be formed.

In this chapter we are going to address some of the common details that people assume you know how to handle—even though you are lost with no guidebook and no road map.

## Custody and Visitation

Custody is not supposed to be about the adults, but for the children. But we adults often make it about us, our schedule, and our needs. In doing this, we fail to realize that even though we want to be with our kids all the time, the kids need to be with the other parent just as much. Except for extreme situations, children should be in both parents' lives on a regular basis.

When making decisions about custody and visitation, we need to ask questions like these:

- What is best for the child?
- How is this helping the child long term?
- How can this be adjusted to be better for the child?
- What message does the arrangement give to the child?

Visitation times are tricky, because you don't want to make your stepchildren feel like they are the visiting outsiders, nor do you want the children who are always there to feel like good things can happen only on the weekends or vacation breaks when the other kids are there. It is in many ways a lose-lose situation. How do you turn it around?

Here are some practical things to keep in mind:

- Don't treat visiting children like guests—they are family.
- Do think of things they might like while there— favorite treats.
- Don't protect them from household chores— involve them in what is appropriate.
- Do ask them to abide by the rules of the house— even if it's only for a few weekends a month.
- Don't fall into the Disneyland Dad syndrome, giving them all you can when they come.
- Do provide appropriate sources of fun and giving—just don't overdo it.

- Don't talk negatively about their other household or family—*ever*.
- Do speak kindly about all their extended relatives when given the chance.
- Don't force them to hang out with stepsiblings.
- Do allow them to plan some of their own activities while with you.

## Family Meetings

A new tradition that I (Debbie) began to dread was the family meeting. The reason I didn't like it was that I felt there was so much emotion, drama, and finger pointing. We adults wanted to create a fair environment, but hurting, confused, competitive children were always drawing lines of comparisons that made it hard to sift through the real stuff. I frequently could feel my "mama bear" suit come on internally and had to fight to avoid defending my own children at every meeting. Far too often the mama bear won out, and I was defensive and frustrated. It was hard to see a solution when I was bent on defending my own kids.

That said, family meetings really are a great tool and should be incorporated into blended families. Remember, most things blended feel foreign at first. Also remember that you are not seeking to live as two separate teams but learning to play on the same team, toward the same goal. Think of these meetings as a team huddle.

Here are some guidelines for effective family meetings:

- Define and confront the issue that is causing the problem.
- Open discussion and allow each person who feels a need to do so to speak.

- Don't force a family member to talk if they choose not to.
- Be ready to compromise.
- Discuss the problem in private when it does not involve everyone.
- Keep the tone calm—no raised voices; don't shout.
- Be sensitive.
- No put-downs.
- Speak toward solutions only. Don't get stuck in complaints.
- Remember to convey love and warmth with instruction and truth.

## Communication Tips for Family Meetings

When *speaking*—

- Don't be afraid to say what you feel.
- Don't give mixed messages.
- Don't presume to read the other person's mind. Ask what they are thinking or feeling.
- Don't become accusatory. Don't berate or speak harshly.
- Do put the focus on one issue at a time.
- Acknowledge your own weakness, and take responsibility when needed.
- Show value to the person you are speaking to.

When *listening*—

- Be attentive and stay calm.

- Keep your mouth shut and listen to what is being said in full.
- Don't interrupt.
- Ask for clarification if you need it.
- Be willing to compromise for the sake of the relationship.

## Holidays

Once you are divorced or widowed, holidays forever change. With remarriage come the immediate relief of family and then the disappointment of not being able to be with your own kids at each holiday. The kids have to be shared, and the parents do the holiday shuffle.

The key to holidays is staying flexible and having the goal of forming new traditions and new norms. Traditions are important, because they build family identity and help everyone involved feel a sense of security. When traditions are changed or broken by divorce, death, or remarriage, something dies inside us. Most of us don't realize how important traditions are to us until something happens to change them and we can't do them anymore.

During the early years of a blended family, there may be positioning to keep traditions alive on both sides. If the traditions of both families are very different, there will always be those who are left feeling like outsiders and struggling with the holidays. Finding common ground for traditions takes time and requires a lot of planning and stretching your flexibility muscles—especially for the adults who are making the plans.

Holidays can overwhelm us with expectations. The members of your new blended family each have their own memories and expectations of what each holiday should look like—and they are all different views. Because of this, not everyone will be happy or comfortable with the new traditions. Holidays evoke strong emotion as there is nostalgia attached to each occasion. When adults refuse to be flexible and insist on their own way, battle lines are drawn.

The relationship with your ex-spouses is put to the test. If you are not in a good place relationally with them and if you are not co-parenting well, don't expect that holiday plans will be easy to work through. That said, even the best of co-parenting relationships have some negotiating to do around the holidays.

Sharing the holidays is a little like sharing the kids. Don't be surprised if your ex does not respect court-ordered agreements. Do everything you can to keep peace, prepare according to the new plan, and then still remain flexible. Here are some of the more common variations of holiday scheduling:

- Every other year—Mom on odd Christmas dates,
  Dad on even Christmas dates.
- 50-50—Part of the time with Mom and the other
  part with Dad. Maybe Christmas Eve with Dad
  and Christmas morning with Mom, or vice versa.
- Early or later celebrations—enjoying the holiday
  a little earlier or a little later that the official date.

At all costs, make sure you are considerate of your children and their other parents as you plan and prepare a new tradition for your own new family. Because holidays are a time to enjoy family and celebrate relationships, be flexible with the ex-spouse's family as well. Grandparents, aunts, and uncles from the previous marriage are not divorced from the kids, so include them in the schedule whenever you can. There are not enough dates to go around, and this can stress out a child if the parent has a negative attitude about it. Go into the holidays peacefully, flexing your grace muscles, and take one date, commitment, and relationship at a time. Teach your children to do the same.

Children need a place to communicate how hard the holidays might feel to them. Although they want to go see the other parent, they may not really feel excited once there. They could feel like an outsider or intruder. Help them to talk through these things, normalizing the situation for them by letting them know that many children are just like them, and it really is hard to shuffle about. Look for the good things to point out, but mainly just make sure your child has a place to be heard.

The first holiday when we didn't have either set of our children was really hard on us. We are both holiday people and love to celebrate, opening our hearts and home. Instead of an old-fashioned family Christmas, by year two we were celebrating just with my (Debbie's) elderly mother. We had a quiet Christmas Eve, and then the three of us opened gifts in the morning. It was weird, and I felt a knot in my stomach the whole time. I longed, really longed, for my kids. After all, it was Christmas, kids are supposed to be with their parents, and ours were—with their other parents.

Here is the truth of it: On some holidays, you will be alone. You can get depressed; anyone would understand. Or you can think of creative ways to make the before or after celebration special—and get over not being with your kids on the actual holiday. Remember—the sadder we are as adults, the harder it will be on children.

## Holiday Meetings

We introduced the family meeting a bit earlier, and now we want you to think about having a family meeting about the holiday plans. Because tradition is important and the entire family has to adjust to something new, try having holiday planning meetings. Make these meetings fun—maybe make some hot chocolate or a favorite dessert—and include a planning board. Make a list of how each family member would like to do the upcoming holiday. You can even make a game out of it. Do this by making some questions, type them, and provide them on cut-up paper strips in a basket. Have each family member draw a question, answer, then pass the basket around for the others. Some of the questions might be:

- What is your favorite thing about Thanksgiving?
- What do you like to do?
- What foods are your must-haves?
- If we had a family party, what part would you like to be in charge of, and why?

Involving the children helps to counteract the sense that their life is totally out of control. Decide to be the adult who promotes peace and who is looking to serve their family during special times.

Here is some food for thought for making holidays work:

- Put the children first.
- Work on merging your two family traditions by keeping something special from each and building toward the future.
- Make plans early.

- Organize details carefully while working to keep things simple.
- Learn to compromise.
- Remain flexible, and be creative when you need to be.
- Let the little things go.
- Make personal sacrifices when necessary.
- Build new traditions with this new family.
- Come up with a plan, and stick to it.
- Be fair and reasonable with gifts.
- Avoid competition.
- Do less, but do what you do more intentionally.
- Put on your best smile, and get along.
- Add new family traditions each year.
- Work on accepting things you cannot change.
- Be careful to check your emotions so that your children won't be so torn between appeasing your emotions and your ex's.
- Remember *why* you celebrate holidays.

Here are some ways to help children honor both families on special occasions, such as birthdays, Christmas, Mother's or Father's Day, Valentine's Day, and so on:

- Take your children to purchase something, even if it's very small, for the other parent and step-parent on special occasions and holidays.
- As children are growing up, allow them the opportunity to pick out gifts for their stepsiblings as well as their own siblings. Make the amounts equal.

- Teach your children to remember birthdays, Christmas, and Mother's and Father's Day for the parents or stepparents they don't live with.
- Let your children know that you have a family budget on holidays and that all children are allocated the same budget when you are purchasing their gifts.

Our family traditions have evolved over the years we have been together. For many of the childhood years, the traditions were fragmented at best. We just had to let go of trying to make it perfect for everyone and work with what we had in front of us. As time has passed and the children have gotten older, we have some definite traditions that they look forward to.

We get together for family birthdays and for Sunday dinner once a month. We also have built a tradition around Christmas where we get together in pj's in the morning. This includes a fire, a short time of worship, hot coffee, and a Cinnabon. Then each person opens a gift one at a time, and afterward we have a family brunch where we share the hardest and the brightest spot of that year and what we hope for the year to come.

We realize that with kids' marriages and grandkids, things will change again. As we said at the beginning, we know we are not the only family, so we must continue to remain flexible.

## Gifts and Other Minefields

A blended family often seems unfair. The parents have the responsibility to treat all children as equals. This equality enables them to grow up with a positive view of themselves, their place in the family, and their value to both their parent and stepparent. This equality is something that should not be negotiable. Each parent must insist that their child be given the same amount of resources as the other's child. Regardless of what is provided for them by the other household, each child notices what the other children are getting and draws lines of comparison accordingly.

I (Debbie) can remember feeling frustrated that Ray and I agreed to spend the same amount of money on the boys' Christmas gifts as on the girls'. To me it wasn't fair, because the boys' father was not in a position to get many things for them, and there was no exchange on his side of the family. That meant that they got far fewer things than the girls did. The girls had their mother, her relatives, and Ray's relatives. In their "other family" they were the only children, and they got double the amount of gifts the boys received.

I realized that when they opened up gifts together it needed to be the same, but I thought that some concession should be made, somehow. I chuckle just thinking of where my head was then. I justified my thought process by reasoning that if we couldn't get something on the girls' wish list, they could get it elsewhere. But if we couldn't get something on the boys' wish list, they just didn't get the thing they hoped for.

How does a child understand that? I kept wanting to make up for what was lacking for the boys, but to do so would mean spending more on them than the girls—and then the girls would know that, and how would that be fair? There was no way to make this fair—at least not in my mind.

Over the years I kept receipts and gift lists, because I knew that given a weak moment, I would be accused of slighting them and not doing the same for them as the boys. I resented this at first but realized it was necessary and still do it, by habit, today.

While I (Ray) understood Debbie's feelings, I felt it was important to be fair with all four children. We could not control what happened on either side of the other fence, so we were just responsible to be fair in our household. This was something that we had to be open about and teach the children. Still, there was some resentment on both sides on occasion—the girls thinking the boys got more, and the boys thinking the girls got anything and everything they wanted because they had another family also buying them things. Keep in mind that in a child's mind, things can equal value and their worth to people. It's important that as adults, we teach them that value attained from getting things is not real value at all.

In the end, it's important for the children to know that in your home each of them is being treated the same way, and each child is valued equally. Do whatever it takes to make that happen.

## Handling Money

Money is a hot topic in blending families. Money is the greatest impediment there is to a decent, well-mannered relationship between ex-partners, declares Patricia Lowe in her book *The Cruel Stepmother:*

> It can, and usually does, embitter in one way or
> another both he who gives, whether willingly or by
> force or law, and she who takes, whether she feels
> it sufficient or is bitter because she must skimp
> to get by. And not only does it so affect the two

principals, but their current spouses, if such exist. Unless all concerned have plenty of money, it may and probably will influence the climate between divorced parents and their offspring throughout the growing-up period. It touches decisions about education, housing, clothing, vacations, the medical and dental services chosen and a whole host of other problems sticky enough in their own right.[2]

A counselor we know who works with stepfamilies is succinct: "The whole issue of money is a nightmare!"

Here are some of the root causes of financial discord in blended families:

- Men who feel they've been "wiped out" by their ex-wife may be unwilling to let their present wife know exactly what the financial picture is.
- Career women or single mothers who have had the autonomy to handle their own financial matters may be unwilling to relinquish that independence.
- A father who feels guilty for breaking up the family may feel that he owes his ex-wife and children more than he can afford, considering his new obligations. He may pay even more than is required by the divorce decree, to the detriment of the new family.
- Either or both wives may have inherited money of their own but refuse to allow its use for the

support of the family, while the husband struggles to meet his obligation.

- Grandparents of one set of children are sometimes well-off financially and bestow luxury on these grandchildren, while the other children (step- or half-siblings) are not getting the nice things the others are getting.

- When there are lavish gifts and trips from a wealthy father, the new stepfather may feel devalued and emasculated and may take his feelings of insecurity out on his wife and stepchildren.

- The new wife may have to move into the house where her new husband lived with his ex-wife, but because of financial limitations, there isn't enough money to redecorate the house, so the new wife feels like an intruder.

- The husband and wife keep all their money in separate accounts, impeding the blending process and impeding family unity and trust.

- The ex-wife lives extravagantly on alimony and child support, while the new wife and children must cut corners just to make ends meet.[3]

In a stepfamily there is no way around it—money has to be discussed. And though it should not be discussed at length with the children, it must at times be discussed to help the children from a different family origin understand that what a child receives from the other household, though it seems unfair, is not unfair. It is simply the other parent taking care of that child. Communication can help to minimize resentment. You can try to be fair, but in the end, step-families have little about them that is fair.

It gets very confusing, doesn't it?

Regarding child support, there is no easy way around the subject. Fathers, the law is the law, and as a father it is your responsibility to support your biological children. It is not your new mate's responsibility; it is yours. And mothers with custody of the children—don't be greedy and hold the law over your ex-spouse's head, but be willing to work out an agreed amount that is reasonable for both parties. It is safe to say that usually what one could get in court far exceeds what any reasonable parent can afford to actually give and still live.

Finally, even in this, think of your children. What is important—your children having every little material thing they want while their father is barely getting by? Or your children having a little less but not having to worry about their father's welfare? Children in a blend already worry and grieve things that we have no idea they are worrying about. Why add something more?

Mothers, by being greedy, what does it teach the children? Yes, there are deadbeat dads, but there are also dads who want to step up to the plate in any way they can, but who are discouraged by ex-wives who knock them down every chance they can with monetary demands from the courts.

We have known of men who can't even afford to rent a room after meeting child-support obligations. Christians need to be willing to make reasonable compromises. God really is our source and provision. We need to trust Him, especially in this hotbed of misunderstanding—money. We need to go back to His words again!

*[Jesus said,] "Give, and it will
be given to you. A good measure,
pressed down, shaken together and
running over, will be poured into
your lap. For with the measure you
use, it will be measured to you."
(Luke 6:38)*

In the end, it's not just the father or children who are hurt—now the stepparent is put in a position of animosity and wanting to hide her own assets. She is left to feel forced to keep her things secret, not even being able to celebrate a raise or employment success, as this would send them back to court!

## Supplying the Need

Though we always made being fair the goal, just as in a nuclear family there were times when one child needed something that the other didn't need. They might need different clothes or things for school. One child needing baseball cleats does not mean all children should get a pair of new shoes. When it comes to need, meet the need; when it comes to gifts, inheritances, college, etc.—be equal, and be fair! And when a child receives something from a relative to whom a stepchild is not related, use the situation as an opportunity to talk about how the children feel.

My (Debbie's) mother used to live with us. We asked her to be fair when all four children were present on holidays, and she respected that. She diligently gave the girls the exact amount she gave the boys. However, if she wanted to do something just for her own grandchildren, we did not rob her of that joy. We asked her to do it on the weeks when the girls were not with us, so that it would not be in their face that she got something special for just the boys. This seemed to work well.

It gets tricky as the children get older and a grandparent from the other side offers to buy them something like a car, or their other parent offers to do so. This happened with our oldest son. Grandma wanted to help him out, but that did not mean we had the resources to help the girls out when they began to drive. What Grandma did put us in a bit of a predicament, and the girls didn't initially understand that up front, and neither did their mother. Left only to us, we would not have been able to buy all four children cars. This is where communication is important, and what comes from you, the parents, is important. The parents must play fair, and then help the children realize that you cannot control what is given from the other side.

## Stay-at-Home Mom—One Couple's Story

Margie is a thirty-seven-year-old stay-at-home mom, with two young children from her first marriage. Her second husband, Dan, has two older children who live out of state. Though Margie has everything she needs, she is still getting back at her ex-spouse for hurting her. She takes him to court whenever she can find a reason to. The judge has given her warnings, and she is coming to the end of her manipulating rope. She tries to squeeze out of him every dime she can—even though she does not need his money.

On the other hand, Margie's ex, Paul, is remarried and has a new child. He and his wife both work full-time jobs, barely make ends meet, and dutifully give the allotted child support, which is 40 per-cent of their take-home income. In addition, Paul gives gifts at every occasion and helps with special things as needed.

Margie is never happy or appreciative. Paul's new wife feels tired and trapped. Margie won't budge and has told the children that Paul always complains about money. Paul is on the verge of giving up and giving in to becoming a fade-out dad.

## Let's Take a Closer Look

### The Problem

A vindictive, greedy ex-wife is using money to punish, rather than to take care of children's needs. This is making the environment hostile and hurting the children long term. Margie is poisoning the kids about their dad, telling them that he is being negative and com-plaining about money.

### The Path

Many men give up on their children, relinquishing them to be raised by stepparents, while they as the fathers begin to fade out of the picture. This usually happens because discouragement is a big part of the blended-family picture for fathers who don't have custody of their children. But Paul cannot give up on his children because of pressure and disrespect from his ex-wife. To fade out now would only prove that what their mother was saying was true. Paul's challenge is to stand up for what is right, support his kids, and keep his hope in the future. This time will pass, but how it is lived now will affect Paul's children for life.

### The Promise

The principle of reaping what you sow should be considered here. If Margie's vindictiveness continues, there will be problems down the road for everyone. She will harm the children by involving them in adult matters.

### The Plan

In order for the two families to get along, there has to be some compromise, but no one has yet been able to get through to Margie. Paul and his wife will need to do a lot of praying in this very difficult situation. They must not allow themselves to lose hope. They must remain united, trusting God every step of the way.

## A Closer Look at All of Us

In recapping this chapter, there are some challenges that we all have in common as adults in the blender:

- Handling money
- Handling holidays
- Gifts and other touchy situations
- Custody and visitation
- Family meetings and resolutions
- Stepparenting hurdles

All of these challenges can bring similar emotions to the surface: anger, frustration, rejection, resentment, bitterness, insecurity, and fear.

Life is full of brokenness. We can't deal with the brokenness without turning again and again to the Father.

### The Problem

We are human and we want our way.

### The Path

There is a way that seems right to us but might lead to more hurt because of our selfishness.

### The Promise

When we acknowledge God, He promises to direct our paths.

### The Plan

We will do better if we lay it all down and allow God to shape us.

## Bringing It Home

- What is the hardest practical area in your attempt to blend?
- Does the fact that your "new" family is already set in some traditions throw you off balance? If so, how have you responded so far?
- How can you begin to fit your life and your traditions into established ones that others have?

- Do you feel you are fair with the children and stepchildren? Explain.
- Who handles the money in your family, and how is it divided? How do you feel about that? Why?

# 8

# **Children Matter**

*Innocent Lives Get Caught Up
in the Blender Blades*

**We simply cannot say we love Jesus
and choose to reject a child.[1]**

I can still recall, as if it were yesterday, the look of horror that filled my oldest son's face when his father and I sat him down for "the talk." That grief-stricken face, and then my son running around the house screaming, "No, no, no!" That kind of sadness doesn't go away overnight. The next snapshot is of a darling tuxedo-clad young boy at his mother's remarriage, pushing me across the dance floor in anger—at the realization that he was not the only one who got to dance with me. As he curled into a corner and cried, my heartstrings snapped a bit. But when something like that happens, you just pick the children up, kiss their cheeks, and everyone moves on. Right?

As adults, we push our children to move on and into new roles, new families, and new lives—sometimes without ever acknowledging their hearts and hurts. Don't get me wrong; I'm not suggesting we don't care, but what I am saying is that I think we have a tendency to minimize the amount of hurt and grieving that goes on in a child's heart. It's time to stop and pay attention and act accordingly. In losing the biological structure of the family, it is possible the children have suffered:

- The loss of security and control over their lives.
- The shock that hope can be destroyed.
- The realization that parents can lie and do hurtful things.
- The insecurity that tomorrow is unpredictable.
- The trauma that God may answer prayer in a way that disappoints us or causes sadness.
- The realization that despite what the pastor says, marriage is not always forever.[2]

There is something happening everywhere—in our homes, neighborhoods, and even churches. Emotional wounding is the frequent by-product of our divorce rate, remarriage rate, and the speed at which new blended or stepfamilies are being formed each day.

The state of the American family is altering the mental and emotional state of our children. While we as adults fight for fairness and try to find our "best life," our children get caught in the fray of our self-focused attempts at moving on. Is this what we want?

A generation of brainwashed children who are comfortable with manipulation, hurt, and lies?

We must wake up to the call of God and handle the innocent lives of children seriously, prayerfully, and responsibly.

What would Jesus say about this type of treatment in the homes of single-parent and blended-family homes today? I think He would not be happy with how we often treat as insignificant the emotional and spiritual lives of little ones He loves. It's clear that children matter to Jesus. He said,

> *Let the little children come to me,*
> *and do not hinder them, for the*
> *kingdom of heaven belongs to such*
> *as these. (Matt. 19:14)*

He said this when children were brought to Him for prayer. The disciples were not happy that the children were brought up to *bother* Jesus, and they rebuked those who brought the children to Him. But Jesus taught us something about the value of a child when He said, "Let the little children come to me." Obviously, Jesus places a high value on children. Do we?

## Respecting a Child's Process

We spoke briefly in an earlier chapter about the grieving that is often present in a remarriage as we die to the dreams of living happily ever after a second time around. Now it's time to turn the attention on the children in the blender and some of the very real grief that they experience—sometimes for many years.

For an adult, a new family is formed. But to a child, it's not a real family but the end of all they hold dear. It is the end of security as they know it, the end of the family as they know it, often the end of their own space in the house or their previous place in the family. Their world has been rocked, stripped, turned over—and we smugly say, "Kids are resilient." Though children will survive, they are not the bounce-back dolls we believe they are.

The loss associated with the death of a parent or the divorce of parents leaves a trail of change that imparts seeds of loss and fear into children. While adults are mature enough to reason things through, children are at our mercy for understanding and help to ease the pain and confusion.

Unfortunately, in this generation of divorce wars, children are often poisoned against parents they dearly love. Confusion sets in, and soon anger and unrecognized stages of grief follow. In an attempt to microwave our lives, many adults move on quickly to the next relationship or the next thing. Though Ray had been divorced for several years, I (Debbie) met Ray rather quickly after my marriage fell apart. In the wave of my own hurt, I didn't consider how soon it was or how that might affect my children. I didn't realize at the time that I hadn't grieved my own losses and my children hadn't even begun to understand theirs.

Most counselors agree that whether the situation involves the death of a parent or a divorce, it would be wise for parents to wait a minimum of two years after the breakup before introducing a new person into the child's life. This helps prevent the short-circuiting of the child's grief process. A short-circuited grief process can affect a child well into his or her adult years.

A wedding, though joyous for the adults, is another life transition that causes sadness for children. Remember, all they ever want is for their "real" family to be back together. Once the wedding happens, the cumulative effect of grief begins to pile on—a move to a new house, sometimes a new city, a new school, new friends, someone else's new cooking, and a new adult to answer to. It can be overwhelming for children. Because they don't have the emotional maturity or the communication skills to express themselves, the state of being overwhelmed with it all gets channeled into acting out, tuning out, or wanting out.

The nature and circumstances surrounding a loss alter the course of the grieving process:

> The more complicated the circumstances, the more prolonged and complicated grieving becomes. For example, the loss over a parent with a terminal illness begins long before the actual death. The unexpected loss of a mother or father killed in a car wreck may extend grieving for many years.... A parental divorce that happens quickly due to an affair affects the kids differently than one in which the couple has been arguing and threatening divorce in front of the kids for years. The children are still deeply affected, but the grief will follow a different course. Researchers have discovered that the negative impact of divorce on children is worse when the parents' marriage had low conflict, as opposed to those with high conflict levels. The former brings

an unexpected and uncontrollable loss, leaving the children to wrestle with the shame of parents who didn't seem to try hard enough.[3]

Stepfamily expert Ron Deal and his coauthor Laura Petherbridge encourage us as parents in these situations to be our children's grief counselors. In *The Smart Stepmom,* they write,

> Permitting sadness and (appropriate) expressions of grief is the foundation for grief counseling. You cannot fix the child's pain, but you can hug it. A small child who falls and skins their knee will most assuredly cry out in pain. Putting medicine and a Band-Aid on the abrasion helps, but affection is what really matters. Holding and consoling the child helps the hurt. It doesn't fix the skinned knee, but the child feels better. In similar fashion you can help your stepchild with the wounds to his or her heart. Allow them to cry over what hurts. Knowing you care is what makes a difference.[4]

Grief is an emotion that demands attention. Ignoring it won't make it go away. In 1969, psychiatrist Elisabeth Kübler-Ross introduced what became known as the "five stages of grief." These stages were based on her studies of the feelings of patients facing terminal illness, but many people have generalized them to apply to other types of negative life changes and losses, such as the death of a loved one or a breakup of a family. These five stages are:

- *Denial:* "This can't be happening to me."
- *Anger:* "*Why* is this happening? This is so unfair! Who is to blame?"
- *Bargaining:* "Make this not happen, and in return I will ____."
- *Depression:* "I'm too sad to do anything."
- *Acceptance:* "I'm at peace with what happened."

As you or your children go through these stages of grief, you probably won't experience them in a neat, sequential order, so don't worry about what you "should" be feeling or which stage you're supposed to be in. Kübler-Ross herself never intended for these stages to be a rigid framework that applies to everyone who mourns. The stages were to be used as a tool to help people understand the grieving process, not a means of tucking messy emotions into neat packages. All losses are different. And, as individuals process their losses in life differently, there is no typical response.

Grief is a roller coaster, not a series of stages, and that roller coaster is part of what makes blending so hard.

## An Advocate for the Children—One Couple's Story

Mary and Ted had been married for five years. It was the second marriage for both of them, and it wasn't going well. Ted had one teenage son from a previous marriage, and Mary also came into the relationship with one teenage son. The boys were eighteen months apart and pretty good friends. But after five years of marriage, Ted and Mary were not too friendly. There was no romance, not much kindness, and their fighting increased by the month.

"If I could do it all over again, I would not marry Ted," Mary mumbled through her tears. "I'm scared, because I have lost feelings for him. Every time he is cruel to my son, it kills part of me. I feel like the man I have committed my life to is slowing cutting away at my heart through his harsh attitude, unloving nature, and unforgiving stance toward a child who is part of me."

Mary went on to explain how years ago her son got into trouble and her husband was unwilling to let go of the offense. Yet when his son did something wrong, Ted was quick to overlook the problem. It seemed to everyone who knew them that Ted was unwilling to even try to love or accept her son. Yet Ted was a deacon at their church, involved with helping people in need, and well thought of in the community. But at home it was a different story.

Ted had also spoken about the marriage and the realization that it was going down fast. When asked why he could not accept Mary's son, Ted just shrugged his shoulders and said, "He's a punk. I have no use for him." When asked about his own son's recent brush with the law, he calmly said, "Everyone gets in trouble from time to time." His inability to see any wrong in his own child along with his swift pointing of the finger at Mary's son altered the balance in their home.

## Let's Take a Closer Look

### The Problem

Ted's love was conditional—based on whatever he felt like giving at the time. The way he treated his stepson was destroying his marriage, his family, and even worse, destroying part of a teenage boy's young heart. Without realizing it, Ted was negatively influencing another human being's self-esteem and opinion of what it means to be a Christian man. This impact could last a lifetime. If Ted continued to reject her son, Mary would have to make the painful decision between choosing to love Ted or choosing to protect her son. This was a no-win situation for Mary.

## The Path

Children need an advocate. Suppose Mary went along with her husband and began rejecting her own son for the sake of a good relationship with her new husband. Where would that leave her son? Without an advocate, the child would be lost and alone in this world.

## The Promise

God promises that we will reap what we sow. If we sow negative judgment into a child's life, we will end up seeing the result of those seeds. On the other hand, if we dare to sow seeds of love, we will see God build up our children, making them strong and fit for life.

> *Do not be deceived: God cannot be mocked. A man reaps what he sows. The one who sows to please his sinful nature, from that nature will reap destruction; the one who sows to please the Spirit, from the Spirit will*

*reap eternal life. Let us not become weary in doing good, for at the proper time we will reap a harvest if we do not give up. (Gal. 6:7–9)*

### The Plan

Innocent children had their lives ripped apart somewhere along the way, and now we as the adults must lead these children in the path of redemption and restoration. It is the responsibility of the adults in children's lives to lead them down a path that will eventually lead them to the love of Christ.

## Children and Change

Tammy was only twelve when her mother remarried and her new stepfather moved into the condo that she and her mother had shared for several years. Immediately it seemed as if Tammy was an outsider. The rules and systems that had been in place with Tammy and her mom were now thrown out the window as her new stepdad reconstructed rules and responsibilities in order to create a home he would be comfortable in. Tammy felt that life began to revolve around a man she hardly knew and that even her own mother put her on the back burner of life.

Tammy's story is a familiar one. Children tell of situations where everything in their lives was changed by moving to a new house or a new school or having to abide by completely new rules. Things as silly as not drinking out of your mother's glass, when you have sipped from her glass your whole life, to no phone calls after 8 p.m., when your previous phone curfew was 9:30 p.m. Think for a moment what these blended families are doing to the children. Imagine walking in their shoes for a moment. It's not a pretty picture.

## Don't Minimize Your Impact

Children are being affected by the actions and reactions of their parents after divorce or in remarried blended-family structures. Dr. Richard Warshak, author of *Divorce Poison*, says,

> The failure of their parents' marriage is a chilling lesson that we cannot always count on love. At such a vulnerable time in their lives, children especially need and deserve as much love as they can get. Those who close off avenues of love and support detour children from their pursuit of emotional security. And when they manipulate children into erecting the barriers themselves, when they enlist them as agents in their own deprivation, they violate their children's trust in a most cruel manner. It is a form of kidnapping; stealing the soul.[5]

We have seen well-meaning adult Christians create havoc in their child's mind. They don't see the long-term impact of what is taking place, so they can easily justify their behavior. Bad-mouthing, brainwashing, and bashing are all things that remain alive and well after divorce. Ex-spouses who live apart from each other hurt their children and jeopardize their emotional health. Toxic criticism maligns parents and destroys children.

Warshak adds, "Experts regard the attempt to poison a child's relationship with a loved one as a form of emotional abuse. As with other forms of abuse, our first priority must be to protect children from further damage."[6] We believe this is the new abuse of our time.

Most of us have to admit that try as we might, there have been times when we have been guilty of putting our children *in the middle*. After all, if we got along with their other parent we would probably still be married to him or her. These relationships are usually awkward at best, and so we must be self-aware and make a commitment to God to not speak about the other parent in a way that would be malignant to our child's heart. Perhaps you can see yourself in the following checklist of malignant motives taken from *Divorce Poison*:[7]

- Poor boundaries—failure to recognize the distinction between the parents' thoughts and feelings and the children's needs
- Desire for revenge
- Narcissism—the drive to magnify one's own importance while diminishing the value of the other parent
- Guilt—the attempt to deflect attention from one's own failings as a parent by denigrating the other parent
- Insecurity—the fear that the children will prefer the other parent
- Desire to vent anger about the ex-spouse and have feelings validated by friends without taking steps to protect children from exposure to criticisms of the other parent

- Unwillingness to accept the end of the marital relationship
- Paranoia—unwarranted belief that the other parent is fostering alienation
- History of a poor or absent relationship with at least one parent

My friend Pam's daughter had a mini meltdown. She had just graduated from college and moved in with her father—a man she hardly knew. One evening she just blurted out the million-dollar question that she had been carrying around for years:

"Dad, how come you didn't want me?"

"Oh, I wanted you, honey, but the courts gave you to your mom."

"No, I mean, how come you didn't want mom to be pregnant with me and weren't happy when I was born?"

Shocked, her father could not believe what he was hearing.

"Who told you that I never wanted you?"

"Mom has always told me that. I have always known the truth."

Now, wiping tears from his eyes, he said, "Sweetheart, I not only wanted you; I loved you from the minute you were born, with all my heart! What you have heard is clearly not even remotely the truth."

For years she had been torn between the father who acted like he loved her and the father her mother painted with her words. Because she didn't live with her father for a large portion of her growing up years, the picture that was painted became the reality of her mind. Believing her father never wanted her was a secret wound and fueled other hurts and insecurities—hurts that will follow her through life.

It became clear that not much she had been told about her dad over the years was the truth. And the negatives were not only hurting a child—they were clearly unnecessary!

## When Do I Speak Up?

Though there are times to be silent when being bad-mouthed, there are also times when it is appropriate to speak up. But before discussing with your children the alleged things that the other parent is doing, you should consider your motives and weigh the potential benefits or risks to the children.

1. What is the real reason for speaking to my child about "this" information?
2. Am I harming my children by my behavior?
3. Do my children hear mostly criticism from me about their "other" family?
4. Do I say or do things that promise the child a reward if they side with what I want?
5. Am I responsible for damaging the biological bond and thus responsible for emotional abuse?
6. If I were still happily married to my ex-spouse and wanted to protect the children's relationship with that parent, how would I handle the situation?
7. Will speaking up to my child in a constructive way help my child?
8. Am I healed enough from the past hurt to be constructive rather than negative?

We personally think that number 6 is a key consideration in handling the children. *What if* you were still married and protective of that parent? How would you handle things? When being real about this, we came to realize that it will not help our children to hear us berate their other parent. And it could undermine respect.

## Life Stages Altered by Remarriage

Ray and I came together with children of similar ages. My older son, Justin, was my firstborn and the leader. Ray's older daughter, Ashley, was the firstborn in her family and clearly the leader. When we got married, Ashley relegated to the number-2 position, and my younger son, Cameron, was no longer the baby of the family, because his new stepsister was a few months younger than he was.

The roles, pecking order, and family structure all changed for these kids once we said, "I do." In the growing-up years, this had quite an impact on the older two—and they definitely had a rivalry going on. Funny thing is, rivalries are not just with the children; the parents and grandparents can easily get just as caught up in it. My older son became the brunt of dislike with his new step-relatives. And I have watched through the years how this affected him. He began withdrawing. No one wants to be around someone who doesn't like them. For children, who just want to be accepted and loved, this is all just too confusing.

In some cases, the children feel divorced from grandparents, aunts, and uncles on the side of the biological parent they no longer live with. Imagine what this is like for the child, who never divorced anyone!

My own children began to be forgotten by their father's family. It's not that anyone meant to leave them out; it just happens. Over time, the cards stopped and the calls ceased. The grief is horrendous for a child, but they don't express it as grief—it comes out in other ways over the course of a lifetime.

Laura Sherman Walters covers this in her book *There's a New Family in My House!*

> All of the literature indicates that children need to mourn longer than we realize, and we must give them that time. Get books to read on the stages of grieving and storybooks for your children, who are not as experienced as you at handling life's hard lessons; neither are they equipped emotionally to deal with pain or make sense of their circumstances.[8]

## Are Children Always Affected?

A blended family is not always a negative in a child's life. But if children are caught up in the cross fire of their parents' fighting, it always affects the child negatively. It hurts to see your parents take shots at each other, and it hurts when you are enlisted in a campaign against one of your parents. Whenever one of the parents wants to turn a child against the other parent, a poison begins to enter the heart and life of the child.

Parents are not the only targets of bad-mouthing, bashing, and brainwashing—even grandparents and entire extended families can receive the same treatment. In all cases, the children suffer.

I (Debbie) have found that most mothers relish the opportunity to make sure the children know that Mom is the good parent and

Dad is now the second-rate parent. I realize I am being harsh here, but stay with me.

Women have a lot of power over their children. And women often do not have healthy boundaries in speech and action in these situations. Why? Because Mom might not have dealt with her own anger or hurt. So without realizing it, we take the hurt and plant it into our children's hearts. Our words and actions will affect our children for a lifetime. Don't be fooled—a biblical principle applies here: You will reap what you sow (Gal. 6:7). If you plant negative seed, in time you will reap a negative result. It might seem to be working for you now, but your children will grow up, and they will end up resenting you for turning their hearts away from their other parent. Please pay attention to this.

## The Heart Struggles We Can't See

When a stepparent moves into a child's life, there is an immediate power struggle in the child's heart. Children didn't get to vote on this new parent, did not have a say in the matter; they liked their old life much better—it was familiar and safe. Many times a new stepparent makes the environment feel unsafe for the child.

Unfortunately, too much energy in the stepfamily gets focused on the adults, when most of the attention needs to be shifted to what is best for the children. God cares deeply about the innocent lives that have gotten caught up in the whirling blades of the blender.

Children are often intimidated by a new stepfather. This is usually because men, knowing they are to be the head of the house, move in and begin changing everything and then enforcing the changes with an iron fist. Maxine Marsolini tells of one such story in her book *Blended Families:*

> He wouldn't even let me use the bathroom by my room. I had to go to the other end of the house and ask if someone was in the bathroom I was told to use before I was allowed in the one across from my room. And ... he felt he could walk in on me anytime he wanted.... I used to play on the lawn, [but] since my stepdad came, I can't even play on the lawn anymore because he thinks I will ruin it.... [S]ometimes my mom prays with me, and she lets me spend a lot of time with my friends.... That way I'm not around the house so much.[9]

Does any of this sound familiar or similar? Most nuclear family structures are set up with the man in control. As stepfathers begin their new role, it is natural for them to try to do what they believe is the right thing and to begin controlling the environment. But this instant change of command is very hard on the children. Many of the studies done on stepfamily relationships suggest that how well a stepfamily member adjusts to the circumstances depends on how issues pertaining to the role of the stepparent are managed. Going about this tall order is where we run into problems. Instilling fear in our children will not be an effective approach. Marsolini explains,

> There is the "Captain" father. He wants to groom a ship-shape family. So from day one he corrects every

behavior he is not pleased with in the children, from how they chew their food to whether they put on a belt with their jeans. If he can just fix the kids, his home will be happy. And his new wife will be so pleased, even proud of him. This doesn't work—probably because he wants respect for rules, not relationship.[10]

## Define Love as Commitment, Not Feelings

When you said, "I do," you made a covenant not just with a new spouse but also with a new family. As a Christian, you must believe that God called you into this new family and therefore has called you to walk in His love toward children who are not your own. They have become your new ministry, so to speak, and as a ministry they become a challenge. You cannot count on your feelings for any type of ministry work, and likewise you cannot trust your feelings to lead you correctly down this path either.

Love is a commitment of our will. The world we live in tells us to "fake it until we make it" if we are going to experience success. But as Christians in the blended family, may we suggest that in regards to your spouse's children, you "faith it until you feel it."

## Living in Love—by Faith

Paul tells us how to think about what is real in order to live by faith: "We do not lose heart.... [I]nwardly we are being renewed day by day. For our light and momentary troubles are achieving for us an eternal glory.... So we fix our eyes not on what is seen, but on what is unseen. For what is seen is temporary, but what is unseen is eternal.... We live by faith, not by sight" (2 Cor. 4:16–18; 5:7).

When it comes to any choice of the spiritual life, we are instructed to live by faith rather than according to what we can feel or see. This is true of loving anyone, including our stepchildren. God has called us to love Him and to love others. The others include your stepchild—annoying as it may seem, you cannot escape the truth that you are called to love someone else's child. Will you obey that calling or opt for the easy way out, loving only those whom you feel like loving, or those who do things just as you would have them done? Can you love someone who doesn't do life your way?

Here are some faith steps of love for a parent in the blender:

- Love your spouse by loving his or her child. When you became one with your spouse, you became united in Spirit to his or her child.
- Honor God by loving your stepchild. This is a new call of the heart.
- Memorize the attributes of God's *agape* love, and ask God to give you the grace to walk in them: patience, kindness, protection, trusting, persevering, believing the best (1 Cor. 13:4–7). God's love never fails, so trust God to work this unfailing love into your heart as a commitment to this child He loves.
- Recognize the truth that this child has been created by God and is important to Him.
- Make a decision of the will to become the child's friend. Becoming this takes time, so just do your part by being friendly and interested in the child.
- Learn to listen to the child—put down your paper,

ignore your cell phone. Give the child undivided attention when he or she is speaking to you.

- Seek to understand the child—where has he or she come from? Is he hurting? Grieving? Lonely? Feeling abandoned? Lost?
- Recognize that you and the child are different—build on any common interest and lay the differences aside. What does he or she like? How can you build the relationship on common things?
- Be willing to invest your time and energy into the relationship. How can you reach out to the children, including them in your world, rather than just being the innkeeper of the inn where they live?
- Give honest praise and encouragement anytime you can. Look for the good; pray about the bad.
- Ask God to give you a heart for the child—this is the miracle that only God can do.
- When things in the relationship are hard, believe that God is shaping and changing you. Walk by faith. Faith steps of love, choices of intentional acceptance, please God.

## Real-Life Family Relationships—Your Story

### The Problem

You don't feel connected to your stepchild. Your feel disrespected by your stepchild. You wish you didn't have a stepchild.

### The Path

Which direction will you choose? Eyes on self, or compassion for a child who did not choose this life?

### The Promise

Jesus honors and cares for each individual life and bids each to come to Him. We are not to turn away the children from God's love.

### The Plan

Find ways to connect. Perhaps the disconnect is your unloving heart and bad attitude. Talk to your spouse about your belief that the child disrespects you, and if there is anything that can be done to instill respect, begin working on it as a couple. Earn a place in your stepchild's life through relationship. Refuse to be negative one day longer. You have a stepchild—now accept it, accept the child or children, and honor God in those relationships. This might turn out to be life's greatest ministry!

In summary, let us not forget that children are children whether they are two or twenty-two. They have family dreams and happily-ever-after dreams of their own. They just want to be loved, and now we have the chance to make a difference.

## Bringing It Home

- Do you have trouble connecting with your step-child? If so, describe the factors that you think contribute to that.
- What could the child do differently that would turn this around for you?
- Because children are affected by your attitude toward their "other parent," when was the last time you spoke well of the other side or the other family?
- When was the last time you spoke negatively?
- What do you think of the term "the new abuse"?
- Do you think that children are expected to just rebound and adjust?
- How can you help be an advocate for the children in the blender?

# 9

# From the Other Side

*Our Children Speak*

**"He restores my soul," wrote the
shepherd. He doesn't reform; he
restores. He doesn't camouflage the
old; he restores the new. He will restore
the hope. He will restore the soul."[1]**

He was grown up. How did that happen? Our first one to leave for
college was back for a visit, and I couldn't be happier.

"Hey Mom, I have an idea for a book!"

"Really?" I asked. "What do you want to write about?"

"It would be called *From the Other Side,* because I think that
adults need to know what it's like being on the other side—having
stepsiblings, not seeing your own father, knowing your real father

has other children living with him while you never see him, trying to figure out loyalties, and stuff like that."

"Oh. Why now?"

"Because adults need to pay attention. Kids are dying inside."

His words got my attention.

When the first kid leaves the nest, it is a little scary. Uncharted parental territory makes anyone nervous. I (Debbie) had no idea how hard it would be to let the oldest go. The apron strings were practically shredded to pieces by the time we made our way to his new home—a dorm room on the Biola University campus. Always the protective mom, I was afraid to leave him there—was he ready? Would old wounds surface? Was he as healthy as he seemed, or would growing up bring out all the ugly stuff that divorces leave in the cargo department of a child's heart?

And just as I had suspected they would, those four years in college opened up many things in my son's heart. The opening of wounds led him to some bad choices and heartbreak. But in the end, he is standing firm in who he is as God's child, learning from his mistakes and seeing how the past has caused him to need the grace of God for inner healing and wholeness. Over the years, the rest of our children have been learning to stand in the position of being restored too.

His idea started something new in our blended-family classes. Now when we teach in our local church, we dedicate one of the evenings to our adult children. Not all of them are there at once, but we usually get a couple of them to come and share from their hearts what it's like to be on the other side of things. We allow the participants to ask questions. Over time, some of the same questions have emerged, and in this chapter we asked our children to answer them for you.

We emailed each of them ten questions and asked them to be vulnerable, open, and real. We are not worried about being exposed, but we are concerned about you, as adults, hearing from the other side, so that you can see the bigger picture.

Let us introduce you to our children with some pertinent background on each one:

## The Boys

I (Debbie) had sole physical custody after the divorce. Occasionally their father lived in our area, and they saw him every other weekend. But for the most part their father, stepmother, and stepsibling lived out of the area, and the boys visited only on some holidays and summer vacation. They have a half-brother from their father's second marriage.

*Justin* was nine years old when Ray and I married. He was hit hard by the divorce. Adjusting to a new environment was hard on him. He quickly took on the role of the "little man" and at a young age was protective of his brother and me. He later became the class clown and the center of attention. This became his coping skill.

*Cameron* was six on the wedding day. He was clueless about the divorce when it happened. He was young, but the impact hit him later, probably in elementary school when he felt different from his friends, because "he didn't have a father." He did live with a stepfather, but to his little boy mind, that was not the same as having a father. In his teen years, music and sports became his solace and songwriting his coping mechanism.

## The Girls

I (Ray) had joint physical custody after the divorce. When I was a single father, they lived at my house every other week. This continued for a few years after I remarried. But when the girls were in junior high, I lost a custody battle, and they moved to Colorado with their mother and stepfather. Once they moved to Colorado, we saw them only in the summer and during the holidays. Needless to say, the move away hugely affected our once closely bonded father-daughter relationship.

*Ashley* was seven years old when Debbie and I married. A classic firstborn, she has always been driven, independent, and protective of her sister. Ashley became her mother's confidante at a young age and then began juggling everyone's feelings, because she tends to feel responsible and wants to make everyone get along or have fun.

*Megan* was five years old when we married. Just a baby when her mother and I divorced, Megan is the one child who has no memory of her parents being together.

Her best friend has always been Ashley, and her blended-family ally in childhood was Cameron. They are just months apart, both were athletes, and they became fast friends. People often thought they were twins. But other than her relationships with Cameron and Ashley, Meg was quiet and kept to herself.

The girls lived with the knowledge that Justin and Cameron were living with me and that I was treating them as my sons, as they themselves lived in another state and were not part of my daily life.

## The Children Speak

### *What has been the hardest thing about being in a stepfamily?*

**Justin (29):** The hardest part for me has been learning to accept my stepdad and my stepsisters as "real" family. It has been a challenge to be close to them and not feel like we are two families but to really accept that we are one big new family.

**Ashley (27):** As a young adult, finding my place in the family— where I fit or what my role is—has been difficult. For instance, my older stepbrother is "the funny one," my younger stepbrother is "the musician," and my sister is "the athletic, tall model." At times I have felt left out, unimportant, or overshadowed as I've tried to find my spot in this blended family. But I think this could be true for intact families and blood siblings as well. One aspect that has been difficult throughout each stage of being a stepfamily has been balancing my parents and the differences that come with their lives (locations of living, personalities, events, families, etc.).

**Megan (25):** It's difficult to state the hardest aspect of being in a stepfamily, since each stage of adjustment and growing leads to a new challenge. When I was younger, being away from one parent for long periods of time was difficult, as was changing households on a weekly basis. In my adolescence, visiting California during the entire summer and being away from my friends and mom was difficult.

**Cameron (25):** Being in a stepfamily is a strange thing. In my experience being blended, I'd have to say that no one thing is harder than another. There are so many dynamics in change, ranging from which kids are at the house on any given week, to which parent is going to discipline me. The hardest part wasn't always a tangible thing, as much as it was the *lack* of an understandable, tangible consistency that I craved.

### Did you miss your father when you weren't with him, living away from him?

**Justin:** Yes and no. For me, my father was a very hard subject and really the most confusing thing that I have ever had to work through. When I was younger, I missed my father, because it feels wrong and weird to have a stepdad, but at the same time I was so hurt by my father that I often didn't miss him.

When he started his new family with my stepmom, stepsister, and new half-brother, I felt as though I did not matter as much anymore, so I checked out, and I really did not miss him all that often. Looking back at the growth that I have had to go through, I can see how I really did miss my father and how I missed out on that very crucial male relationship. Sure, my stepdad was there to fill those shoes, but I could never bring myself to allow him to be that father figure to me 100 percent, so I missed out on a father-son relationship to the degree that I, as a boy and teen, needed that more than anything.

**Ashley:** I did miss my father when I lived away from him. Often

I felt left out of his life with my stepmom and stepbrothers. Although we spoke weekly, when I would come to California to visit, I always felt like I wasn't completely a part of "their" family. I missed out on the day-to-day stuff that you can't always catch someone up on over the phone, and it was obvious when I came to visit.

**Megan:** I missed my dad more than anything. I get choked up just thinking about it. I always felt like I was missing out on getting to know him as my dad, growing up. I would look at other girls and long for my dad in my day-to-day life. I constantly wondered if I would ever have that kind of close relationship with my dad that other kids my age had. I remember feeling left out a lot, because we lived so far away from my dad. For example, in high school we had a fashion show every year to raise money for after prom. Every year the girls walked down the runway in their prom dresses with their dad. The dads would give their daughters flowers at the end of the runway, and I remember how left out I felt, because my dad wasn't there and I still had to walk down the runway with either my mom or a best guy friend, neither of whom could touch not having my dad there. It made me miss him more than anything.

I also remember missing him so much that I developed a fear that I would never have a close relationship with him and that he would die before this could happen. It actually was a big fear that carried into college and even until I moved to California. It was a paralyzing fear for quite some time. Thankfully, God answers prayers and has brought me to California to develop a close and loving relationship with my dad, dissolving my fear.

**Cameron:** I would have to say that I missed my father as much as I knew how to. I admired my dad greatly as a child, but his image wasn't something that I could touch or deeply connect with. He was more like Michael Jordan. Someone who I considered to be a winner, a hero to chase after.

## What do you wish your mother had done differently?

**Justin:** I wish that I had not seen my mother fall apart as often as I did in the early stages, because I felt like I had to be the one to comfort her since dad was gone.

The biggest thing that I wish she had done was say no to me more after the divorce. I think that she allowed me to learn terrible money and spending habits during the time immediately following the divorce by allowing me to get whatever I wanted when we went to the store: toys, candy, video games, etc. There were some limits, but I think that she was trying to get us what we wanted to try and compensate or to give the message, "I'm sorry that this all happened."

**Ashley:** I wish my mother had not shared so much of the adult information with me, such as money issues, conflicts, scheduling difficulties, her negative feelings, etc. As a child, I could not process this information in the proper way, and it affected my relationships with my father, stepmom, and stepbrothers.

I also wish my mother had not turned so frequently to involving lawyers and the courts. It complicated matters and made them so much more hurtful and finalized for me. As an adult, looking back at some of those times, I feel sad for myself and some of the childhood innocence I missed out on. Since I knew a lot of the grown-up information, I grew up quickly and formed prejudged ideas about my stepfamily that, had I not known that information, I probably would not have.

**Megan:** I wish my mom had done a lot of things differently. For starters, I think the most important thing she could have changed was not to talk negatively about my dad and other family to my sister and me. If I could tell parents of divorce just one thing, this would be it: not to talk badly about the other parent. Save it for your counselor, mentor, or spouse, but don't influence your kids to believe what you believe to be true. Let them form their own opinions. Because my mom did this, it gave me a lot of untrue and jaded perspectives about my dad and blended family that have carried over into my adult life, because I believed my mom.

As a kid, you can't separate the pain that a parent feels from what you feel about your other parent. You are too young to understand the difference and sort through what is true and false. It is hard as a kid to make your own opinion about the divorce and certain disagreements, because you trust what your parent tells you is the truth. You don't expect them to deceive you, and you can't understand that their hurts about your other parent are not your hurts or burdens to carry as your own and that you must make your own opinion about it.

I also think that not talking about money issues and court orders with my sister and me was something that my mom could have done differently. Often, I think parents forget that kids are just that—kids.

They shouldn't be brought into the battle that wasn't their choice to fight in the first place.

My mom was also quick to tell my sister and me not to tell our dad certain things. This could range from something as simple as a shirt she bought us to something as big as the fact that she and our stepdad were getting a divorce. This made my sister and me feel trapped, like we could never go to our dad about anything that was really going on. We were raised in secrets and lies, told to keep things from our dad and family that should never have been kept. Even though we were technically two different families, if you look at the big picture, the two families are so intertwined because of the kids and should almost be looked at as one. What happens in one family that involves the child should not be kept from the other family.

I think the most important thing to remember is that what parents model, kids will eventually reflect in their own lives and especially as adults. I think this is true in intact families too, but it has longer lasting effects in children of blended families, because their hurts are deeper and more complex than those whose families are still intact.

**Cameron:** I wish that my mother had told me to remember to appreciate my stepfather, Ray. I was told to respect his rules, his provision, but it was never impressed on me that he was a man to be respected for who he is. I wish I had been told that a father isn't necessarily biological, but a man that God puts in your life to teach you what it means to be a man and how to handle things correctly. The things that only an older wise man can teach you aren't necessarily restricted to biological fathers. Hopefully, men understand the impact of their actions.


### What do you wish your father had done differently?

**Justin:** The biggest thing that he could have done was apologize and explain what happened and why it happened. I grew up just wanting to hear him say that he was wrong in his actions. The next thing is, I wish he would have realized that having another baby was a threat to how we felt about his commitment to us. I think if he had realized this, seeing it from a child's perspective, he would have tried harder to stay in one place—being closer to us, doing whatever it would have taken to be near us, even if that meant that he had to work harder to do so.

**Ashley:** I wish my father had not pushed my stepmom and brothers on me as much as he did. Although his intentions were good, it made it awkward and forced, instead of natural and within my comfort zone. I also wished my father had plugged in more to my life. Even as a young adult, I still crave that time with him, and I think it's natural for a child to crave that time with the parent they are not with. When I say plugged in, often I felt my relationship with my father was surface (partly due to living states apart), but I often felt as though my dad didn't understand my life or who I was or what I was about.

**Megan:** I wish that my dad had been a part of our lives on a daily basis. Although we lived in another state and it wasn't possible, it would have been great to have phone calls more than twice a week. I know that he tried his best to make an effort, considering the cost of phone calls and different schedules, but even coming home to a voice mail from him letting us know he was thinking about us would have meant the world. As a kid, you think that he isn't calling because he is more involved with his new family and kids and that he doesn't have time for you. As an adult, you know this isn't the case, but kids don't understand that. They are self-consumed.

Another thing I wish my dad had done differently is to make my sister and me feel more a part of the blended family when we were growing up. I can't say we weren't included in things, because we were, but I can remember family fights where I left feeling like he chose his new family over my sister and me and that if he had to choose between them and us, he would choose them. I laugh at this now, because it's pretty absurd, but as a kid this is how I felt. Remember, as much as a kid can say they understand or how mature you may think they are, they are still just kids with limited knowledge, life experience, and personal relationships.

**Cameron:** Nobody is perfect, but there are some things that fathers should strive toward. One very important goal should be to run toward selflessness. God has shown us what selflessness looks like in the most intensely beautiful way. I wish my father, who was and still is a believer, had understood that God is very intentional in always being selfless toward us, and He expects us to turn around and do that for our sons. Even if he was in a loveless marriage, he should never have put his family aside in search of personal fulfillment. God doesn't cast us aside, turn His attention away, and focus on flights of fancy. I wish my father, who reads the Bible, had taken note of God's actions toward His children.

## What could your stepparent have done to help you feel more secure in the adjustment?

**Justin:** I don't think that there was anything that he could have done for me that would have changed my security in the adjustment. My father's actions hurt me and created a deep cut in my trust for male figures in my life, and unfortunately my stepdad fell victim to my hurt despite his amazing efforts. I know that my stepdad was not perfect, but I think that he tried and did everything that he could for me as his stepson.

**Ashley:** Early on in the blended-family situation, a lot of things were going on (court battles, accusations, etc.), and I know lots of things were thrown at my stepmom and emotions were high. At times I felt at fault for those things. I felt that way because of my stepmom's reactions or feelings.

When I was younger, I internalized her mood, since at times tensions were so high between my mom and dad/stepmom. For instance, if my stepmom was happy, that meant she liked/loved me or I was doing something right, but if she was quiet or sad, she didn't like/love me and I was doing something wrong.

One thing I think my stepmom could have done to make me feel more secure in the adjustment to the new family was balance or conceal her hurt emotions, as they strongly affected me (remember,

I knew a lot of the adult info from my mom, so I read into my step-mom's emotions and took responsibility for them).

**Megan:** This is a tough question. I think as a kid you fantasize about all the things a stepparent can do to make it better, and as an adult you realize that it's more difficult than you once thought. I think that as a stepparent, you have to fully accept and love your stepkids as your own, as if you are adopting these kids by choice. Kids are more intuitive and perceptive than they are given credit for, and they know if a parent doesn't fully love and accept them. They can see it in your eyes, and they can feel it in your actions.

I think that if my stepparent had set aside one-on-one time with me, it would have been really helpful for me growing up. I was always the quietest kid in the family, which was hard, because I wasn't about to compete for attention from my family, especially from a stepparent, but if my stepparent had sought me out more, it would have meant the world to me. I think that developing bonds from the onset is of upmost importance, because it can only continue to grow. It is much tougher as an adult to build a relationship with a stepparent that you don't feel like you ever knew very well.

I also think that it is important not to take "blood sides" in fights. I remember a few times when our blended family was divided based on blood. It didn't matter who was right or wrong, but it came down to who was your blood parent or child over something as silly as whose turn it was to clean up the dog poop. If you can avoid those situations or be aware of your natural bias, I think that is really helpful. When you make a kid feel as if it is a real family and they are as much a part of it as you say they are, they will eventually feel a part of it. If there are divisions and sides, a kid feels pushed away and is less likely to feel close to a stepparent.

I think it is important for stepparents (and kids) to remember that relationships don't happen overnight. Just like any other relationship, it takes time, trust, and effort. Your stepchild may not fully appreciate what you do for them now, but they will carry those memories of what you did do for them into their adulthood, and it will enhance your relationship later in life.

**Cameron:** I'm not sure there is much that could have been done. Is there a right way to explain to a five-year-old that their family has a rotating cast? Could you even find the words for a ten year-old? I've spent so much of my young life "adjusting." To this point my life has been a series of adjustments, figuring out what my parents gave to me through their divorce. The only thing that can make me feel secure is to look at Christ and His perfection. When everything is broken in my life in some way, Christ is my picture of completeness. And second, it helps to be encouraged into exchanges of love between myself and my parents. Love is an action that is fostered, not just words spoken. To be shown love and treated in a fashion that is *agape* love, or a love of choice. To be shown that my parents' love is consistent, without fear of it disappearing!

## What do you wish had been different for you?

**Justin:** I wish I had been forced to go to counseling to help me talk about my hurts and feelings. I needed help, and it was always an option instead of a mandatory thing.

**Ashley:** I wish my mom and dad had gotten along better when I was younger. I wish they didn't have to solve issues through the courts and had settled them between themselves. This would have made things more manageable and would have created less tension between the two families (which often I felt in the middle of).

**Megan:** Looking back, I don't think that I would wish for anything different. I think our lives are testimonies to the good work that the Lord accomplishes in His time and not our own. I don't think we would be where we are today if we hadn't faced all of the trials and tribulations we did. I think that our lives and our family as a whole went through what we did so that we could be what we are today and so that the Lord could use our family to touch others' lives.

   If you look at the bigger picture, prayers have been answered, our family has been strengthened and made into one, and we continue to be a testimony to other families going through the same thing. I would face it all again knowing that the Lord has used it for good to touch the families He has, and that He has ultimately worked in my life to make me who I am today. I am thankful for who our blended family is today, and I would not trade what we've been through for anything else. These hardships we've faced have shaped me into who I am today, and because of them I think my future family will only be stronger.

**Cameron:** I wish that I had known what it was like to have my father in the crowd at my Little League games. For him to show up. Sometimes I just needed someone to show up for me, to swing the bat with me, to cheer for me. My blended family did this for me, but it always seemed like a consolation prize. My best friends' dads were giving them high fives after games, and all I could do was look at my stepdad, and it felt like a friend was congratulating me. I wish I had understood then that Ray was everything a father is. I was just too young to see it.

## Do you still feel awkward with the family structure?

**Justin:** I would say that I don't feel as awkward as I used to, but I still do feel a little awkward with the structure of the blended family. I think that this is because we have not really been all together as a family until the last four years, so there is a lot of learning that is going on among all of us.

I think that the blended-family situation/structure can make it hard to feel like a cohesive group sometimes, and I feel like we have never really grown as close as most non-blended families are. Sometimes I feel like there are still two "teams," especially when we get in arguments or when problems arise. I am becoming more comfortable as time goes on.

**Ashley:** Although our family has been blended for twenty years, I still feel awkward with the family structure at times. Our family has come a long way and has overcome many challenges, but at times there is still that elephant in the room that we are not blood related. It's hard to explain in words, but there are those moments when it just feels different from what an intact family would feel like (I am assuming, since I don't know what that is like). Or for me, I feel awkward when a conflict arises and I try to solve it.

I always try to be careful not to say too much or dive into an old issue or hurt or make too many waves, almost because I don't feel completely comfortable or safe to say exactly what I am feeling or what is on my mind.

**Megan:** Occasionally, yes. I think that when you are in a blended family there will always be moments of feeling awkward, even as an adult. I think that some of what you felt as a kid carries over to what you feel as an adult, and this plays a role in family structure. These feelings of awkwardness will always need to be assessed and reflected upon, so that you grow out of them or can change the way you feel.

Although I feel more secure in my role in my blended family, there is still some degree of give-and-take and figuring out where you should be in certain situations. It is easy, even as an adult, to revert into how you felt about your blended family as a kid, and it takes conscious effort not to fall into that trap.

**Cameron:** The family structure is always a little awkward at times! Even in families that stick together! I'm not sure if my feelings are due to my broken background, or because that's just how families are sometimes. My guess is that sometimes it's just tough being in a family. But there are times that I withdraw without any reason or understanding. There are times that I just feel like an island. I'm not sure if this is normal or just something I've felt since childhood. I felt I had to mature quickly in life emotionally and mentally, and maybe those feelings have to do with that process.

## What helps you feel secure in the family?

**Justin:** I know that we all love each other even if it doesn't feel like we are all very close at times. I know that we would all do anything for one another in a time of need. To know that everyone's anchor is in Christ makes me secure in where our hearts are for one another. Truthfully, my relationship with my mother makes me feel more secure in our family, because I turned to her when I was younger, so I guess it is my "safe" relationship.

**Ashley:** For one, the stability of this family. As I said, it's been twenty years as a blended family, and it helps to know that we have been together that long and that no one is going anywhere. Funny enough, conflict helps me feel secure, because once the issue is settled, I feel closer to the person/people, which leads to a more real and personal relationship.

The other thing that helps me feel secure is my continued developing relationships with all family members, both blood and step! As we kids have become young adults, our relationships have changed for the better. Our relationships are more intentional, whereas before it was because our parents were married. But now I truly feel connected with all my siblings.

**Megan:** I think the biggest thing that helps me to feel secure in the family is being included and reminded that I am loved on a daily and continual basis. My family was always great about treating us kids as equals, and what they did for one kid they would do for another. I think that's important in a blended family, because it makes the children feel as if there is security and stability, and as if their role is just as important as everyone else's.

I also felt more secure in my family as I understood that my family really knew who I was and how I was different from the other kids in the family. My family has been great about seeing the strengths, weaknesses, and differences in each of us kids, and I think that is really important. I also think that knowing my dad is still my dad no matter what makes me feel secure. I never lost him to a "new" family, and knowing he is always there makes me feel secure. In the same respect, knowing that I have another parent (Deb) to turn to in time of need also makes me feel secure.

**Cameron:** I feel secure when my family is being vulnerable with me. My parents have built a culture in our home of sharing, of wearing your heart on your sleeve. When you are emotionally aching, the worst thing is to hold it in, because it's a wound that festers. But when I know that there is an opportunity to bring that wound out and get some healing, and that everyone else will listen and not judge me for it, then I feel like I'm a part of something!

## What is it like being thrown into a family with other kids and being told they are now your brothers or sisters?

**Justin:** It is terrible!!! It is like someone grabbing two strangers and telling you that now you need to love them because we love each other. It's weird, uncomfortable, awkward, and just plain hard. Not to mention that as the oldest, I then had to compete and fight for my position as the oldest with somebody else who was used to being the oldest. I think that the sibling thing is one of the hardest parts of this situation.

I still struggle with these relationships and being close to the others. As a side note: Having a half-brother enter the scene when I was younger was really hard, because I felt like my dad was saying that we weren't good enough for him, so he wanted to replace us. It has been very hard for me to reach out and be close to my half-brother because of my feelings of hurt that his birth brought. It's not his fault, but sadly, he has reaped the hurt of my heart over the years.

**Ashley:** Once the honeymoon period of being a family subsided, it was tough. For me, I felt a lot of jealousy, confusion, frustration, etc. I went from being the oldest to being the second oldest, and to be quite honest, that didn't sit well with me!

Often I also felt misplaced. For instance, Justin was the oldest, and then Cameron and Megan were the youngest and practically best friends. I felt like I didn't fit, when before I was the oldest and had a spot or role. Not until the last four or five years have Cameron and Justin truly felt like my brothers. I used to refer to them as my stepbrothers, but now when I talk about them to people I say "my brothers." And I truly feel that way. It's amazing how God worked it all together for good and changed it all around! I can't imagine not having Justin and Cameron in my life now.

**Megan:** Depending on your age, at first you think it is really fun. I was five, and what five-year-old would not think it was cool to have two new brothers to play with? The older you get and as time goes on, the more real it gets that these new siblings are here to stay and aren't just built-in playdates.

Being thrown into a new family and being told you have new brothers and sisters is an adjustment and takes time to understand and grasp. These other kids, who were once just your playmates, are now your roommates competing for the bathroom, the TV, and your parent's attention. It is a difficult adjustment, and you can't expect that all of your kids will get along or will adjust the way you want them to, but you can only hope and pray that they do.

I think as a kid, a hard part about this is explaining to people who these other siblings are. You don't want to use the word *step,* because you feel as if that somehow discredits the relationship that has been built, but at the same time other people don't understand your family dynamics if you just call them your brother and sister. To this day when I don't use the word *step,* I still get questions like, "Are you twins? Who is adopted? How did your mom have so many kids so close in age?" It can be quite comical, but it can also be frustrating.

**Cameron:** It's like living with aliens that you get along with! You may really like them, maybe even laugh with them and enjoy their company, but at the end of the day you can't help but think, *I'm so different from them.* Imagine if you walked down the street with a friend, and they grabbed a total stranger and said, "You guys are gonna be roommates forever! You can't refuse! Now go play nice, because now you're also best friends!" Strange thought, right?

## *If you could voice something to parents in blended families today, what would you say to them?*

**Justin:** This was not your child's choice, so *do not* expect them to be excited for you or to love your "new" family immediately. Make the kids go to counseling, and let them say whatever they want without getting in trouble. They are hurt, and if you have started a "new" family, you have made it seem as though you are not hurting and that you are happy now. This creates the pressure to be okay. Also, don't allow them to use their hurts as excuses for bad behavior or acting out when they want their way. Again, I stress the need for counseling.

**Ashley:** Kids pick up on a lot!!! They are smarter and more intuitive than you may think. Keep them out of the adult stuff—don't share that with them. Be honest with them, but edit the stuff they don't need to know and make it "kid friendly."

If possible, try to have a working relationship with your ex. Your kids will truly benefit from this. The less conflict/drama/judges/lawyers/courts involved, the better for the kids and everyone involved.

Check in with them; ask how they are feeling, doing, what they think about everything, how they feel about the changes, etc. And most importantly, just *listen!!!* Don't defend or explain or make excuses—just hear them out. They need a voice too, especially in a situation where they had *no* say.

**Megan:** I would tell them to keep on keepin' on! It is worth the battle to become one family. The Lord is good, and He does work all things together for good. I think that our family is a great testimony to that. If we can make it, so can you!

Remember that no family, blended or intact, is perfect. Consistency and openness to try new things in regards to your blended family will only be beneficial to you and your children.

Above all else, remember that whether your kid is two or eighteen, they are still just a kid, and as much as you think (or they think) they understand divorce and blended families, they don't. You may not see the immediate effects of divorce in your kid, but trust me, you eventually will, and your kid will probably have to process and deal with more than you have had to.

Even at twenty-five, I am still processing and realizing things about myself that are effects of divorce and my experience in a blended family, and I think that these things will affect me for a lifetime. I will constantly have to work on the effects of divorce and how it plays into my relationships, choices, and walk with the Lord. I think that my parents (Dad and Deb) have been helpful in this because of their openness and honesty in regards to our family and divorce. Your kids are eventually going to have questions about why the divorce happened, and I think that being open, honest, and taking personal responsibility will help your children deal with and process the divorce for themselves.

Lastly, be careful about the expectations that you set for your kids in regard to the new family. Remember that it is just as much of an adjustment for them as it is for you. In fact, it's probably a bigger adjustment, because now they have not only one but two families that they have to understand and live with. What you feel about your blended family may not be what they feel, and I think it is important for them to be able to express that.

**Cameron:** Children are a blessing from God. In His Word, He speaks often and intensely about His love for them. If you want your family to work, it's time to start putting your children's needs at the front of your heart. You and your new spouse need to understand that no matter how your children deal with their feelings, they didn't ask for this setup. Practice patience, selflessness, mercy, and compassion. Remind yourself that your children have wounds they never asked for. Divorce can make adults more selfish after remarriage, so guard yourself against life being about *just* you and your new spouse and *your* happiness.

## From the Parents' Side

As you can see, we are not the perfect-specimen parents or stepparents. We have found this journey to be a mix of hard and smooth, ugly and beautiful—good and bad. We have raised this family, and now our hearts' goal is to encourage others who are at home with little kids, hurting hearts, and futures big and bright ahead of them. Like us, you are the adults. Our word to you would be to *be the adult.* By that we mean, put yourself aside when necessary, love the children more intentionally, make peace with your ex readily, and remain flexible. The children are counting on *you.*

# 10

# Help! I'm the Mom in This Mess

## The Traps That Women Can Fall Into

Worldly philosophy is forced to
minimize difficulty because it has no
real answers. But you and I know better
than small-stuff philosophy. We face a
lot of big stuff out there. Only through
prayer are we washed with peace.[1]

Let's face it: Women can be drama. From the time we are little girls
telling secrets to our friends, to the time we are mothers, stepmoth-
ers, and ex-wives, we can be trouble if left to our own ugly selves!

I am convinced that a woman has great influence in her home,
and I am certain that God created us as mothers to have tremendous

sway over our children's and families' lives. Because of this, no matter what kind of a mess my blended family has been, I have felt a responsibility to seek out God's way and God's help in the middle of it all.

When Mother Teresa received her Nobel Prize, she was asked, "What can we do to promote world peace?" She replied, "Go home and love your family." And that is what God calls us to do! Someday your children will grow up and want answers about life. They will struggle with things like identity, the love of God, and the purpose of living. Like us, they will face their own battles with self-esteem and securing their place in the world. Wouldn't it be nice if we were prepared to give them answers? It starts with us as moms. My friend sent me this email, outlining the amazing role of motherhood:

> *Women do more than just give birth. They bring joy and hope. They climb into a person's life and make everything a little better, bringing out the best in their husband, children, and friends. They are the cheerleaders and teachers of America ... the influencers that shape the world. As mothers they are in a partnership with God, working with the Creator of the universe in shaping human character.*
>
> *Have you seen the spec sheet on her?*
>
> * *She has to be completely washable, but not plastic*
> * *Have 200 moveable parts, all replaceable*
> * *Run on black coffee and leftovers*
> * *Be able to feed a family of six on a pound of hamburger*

- *Have a lap that can hold three children at one time and that disappears when she stands up*
- *Have a kiss that can cure anything from a scraped knee to a broken heart*
- *To do her job a mother must be able to multitask*
- *She needs six pairs of hands and three pairs of eyes.*
- *She must learn to wipe a tear, cover a cut, and pat a back at the same time.*
- *She rushes to school to pick up a sick child, sticks notes in lunch boxes*
- *Encourages a child who is sad, lonely, or afraid*
- *Gets excited with a child who has passed a test, or received good news*
- *She spends her life going to school meetings, scout meetings, and carpooling.*
- *She plans birthday parties, graduation parties, and wedding celebrations.*
- *Women carry children*
- *Carry hardships*
- *And carry burdens*

*Yes, a mother has quite a job:*

> *Her job is to take care of the possible*
> *And trust God with the Impossible.*[2]

## Mother to Mother—Stepmother to Stepmother

If I could write a letter to you it might go something like this:

*Dear Mom,*

*You have tremendous power. Your power can be used to shape your children into men and women of faith—men and women who love and serve others and make the world a better place. But your power can also have the opposite effect. Your power can be used to shape your children into bitter, narcissistic, lying, fault-finding men and women. Men and women who do not trust people, God, or life. Men and women who spend the rest of their lives as victims to the lies they have been told, the secrets they have had to keep, and the burdens they should not have had to carry.*

*Please make a difference and use your power wisely.*

In the rest of this chapter I want to address these three topics:

- The way we, as women, represent our children's father to them
- The fact that we, as new wives, are now connected to a wife-in-law
- The ten top mistakes I made, and why

## What Kind of Picture Are You Painting of Daddy?

Like most ex-wives, I was not thrilled with my children's father at the time of the divorce or anytime soon afterward. As he was not living near us, the children only saw him on occasion, and that was fine with me. To my surprise, the children missed him more than I could imagine, and even though he wasn't physically there for them, he always had a piece of their hearts.

The natural tendency that I have seen with women like myself is to try to pry that piece of heart away from the children, so that we feel we are the winner and the children need us and love us most. I realize we don't admit this, but let's face it, girls—it's true! Sadly, when we do this, we are hurting the little people we love most: our children. God set up the family structure, and like it or not, your ex-spouse is in your child's life by divine appointment. Now it's up to you to preserve and protect that.

If you are anything like me, you might be thinking—*What, up to me? No way!*

But if you have the main custodial rights to your children, you are making your mark on them. If you lead them down a path of disliking and dishonoring their natural father, you are operating against God's will and directly against one of the commandments!

> *"Honor your father and mother"—*
> *which is the first commandment with*
> *a promise—"that it may go well with*
> *you and that you may enjoy long life*
> *on the earth." (Eph. 6:2)*

So here's the deal—it doesn't matter what you think of your ex, God thinks that ex is your baby's daddy, and that is a position to be honored. I have heard many women say that their child's father is just a "sperm donor." What a sad statement of not understanding the value of both man and woman—mother and father.

For me the key was implementing Philippians 4:8—"If anything is excellent or praiseworthy—think about such things." I began to identify the things that were good and honest that I could tell my children. I can remember being so wounded by the divorce that I could not muster up the good things very easily. But one thing I did know was that he was a good musician, able to play any instrument by ear—excellently; a true gift from God.

Every time the boys wanted to talk about their daddy, I would say, "You know, your dad is such a good guitar player," or "Your dad is such a good musician." They loved to ask questions about that, and I could honestly and without any tension talk about that as long as they wanted. And guess what? They both grew up to believe that maybe they, too, could learn music, and today both are talented musicians!

Implementing Philippians 4:8 toward my ex-spouse helped me stay positive and steer clear of the negative that would have been so easy for me to fall into. And in time, this positive talk about their dad helped me move into forgiveness and restoration of relationship. After all, just because our relationship didn't work doesn't mean he is a terrible person. There does not have to be a winner and a loser. That competitive mentality will not lead to peace but to more bitterness—ending up hurting the children. Truth is, he is a person just like me—imperfect, made mistakes, needs grace. Children need to know that truth. It will take them far in life.

Don't be responsible for walking away from truth by disobeying the commandment and leading your children toward dishonoring their father. Help them turn the corner, make the change in attitude, and be blessed in doing so.

## There Is Another Woman in Your Life—the Wife-in-Law

Call her friend or call her foe—but don't try to get rid of her, because she is here to stay. Some women get married and think that they will have nothing to do with the husband's ex-wife. That might work if you are not in the children's lives much. But if you are involved in the kids' lives, you will interact with their parent.

When that interaction is with an ex-wife, it could feel like she is the "other" woman in the marriage. Territorial women don't like this much, but let it go and get on with living life to the fullest in this new dynamic. She is not your enemy. She can be your friend. She is, like it or not, now by marriage connected to you because you share the raising of her children. Learn to love her, and refuse to leave her. She is too important to the children's happiness for you to pretend she does not exist.

I personally did not want to be in my wife-in-law's life. Well, I did at first, but our relationship became difficult, and I wanted to run. I was thrilled when a counselor told me that I didn't have to have anything to do with her. Yeah! So I tried that, and the girls hated me more as the days went by. They seemed to do much better when their mother and I were on good terms. I should have gotten a clue, but I am slow, selfish, and stubborn.

Once I began getting over myself, I began trying to develop some kind of relationship, to whatever degree I could, with the wife-in-law. I would suggest you do this too. I am not saying you have to be best friends, but you are connected, so make that connection work for you and the kids. And, like me, you might end up finding a delightful relationship with her. She might even become someone you enjoy seeing when family connections warrant it.

Now that the kids are grown, there isn't much interaction. But when there is, ours is very warm and supportive. Believe me on this—when you give something to God and desire to line up with His heart, He honors that and changes things. Your ex is not your enemy and neither is your wife-in-law. Both are people God loves dearly.

A few months ago, Ray's ex-wife sent me a very touching email. Because we have had a rough road and a hard relationship at times, I will always treasure this email, as I have grown to love and treasure her. I am humbled by her words, because I have made many mistakes over the years. This email is a testimony of how God changes things.

> *Good Morning Debbie…. Thank you for your sweet message. Yes, WHO would have thought years ago that today we would be in this place with each other. I happen to know it is God's plan as to where we are with each other today, and that we grow and forgive. We see things differently too as we get older. I wish I had worked harder at our relationship … but I did make mistakes, and hopefully, learned from them. You truly are a gift to me (and ALL of us), and I thank you for you. Trust me, prayers can't hurt.*

*Anyway my dear ... I am a woman WILD in my faith and loving every minute of it ... and, I love my life. And I thank you for all that you have brought to my life.... Love u, Debbie ... truly. Have a blessed, beautiful day.*[3]

If I had to make one strong recommendation, it would be the book *The Smart Stepmom* by Ron Deal and Laura Petherbridge. I highly recommend the chapter "Meet Your Ex-Wife-in-Law." Good information.

## My Top Ten Mistakes

Naturally I made more mistakes than these, but these are some of the things I did that didn't work and made things worse.

**1. I assumed we would be just one big new, happy family.**

I wanted to pretend we were all together from the beginning— kiss, kiss, love, love. The fact that this wasn't automatic dashed my dreams, and the disappointment almost killed my desire to try to work things out.

**2. I pretended that I was the real mom.**

I cried when my husband proposed to me. They were tears of joy because I loved him and tears of joy because I had always wanted little girls, and now I would have two. But these girls were not my daughters, and I had to learn to balance what it meant to be a step-mother and not the real mother. They have a real mother, and part of my role was to support her role in their lives.

**3. I pretended that my children's stepdad was dad enough for them.**

I wasn't too upset that my ex wasn't around much, because I believed that Ray could be their new dad. How ridiculous of me to think I could just X out the real dad in favor of my new husband. Bad idea, bad plan, wrong way to live. My sons needed their father— still do, always will.

**4. I relinquished discipline of my natural children too soon.**

Let's face it—what single mom doesn't want some help? Not so quick! Your children will be shell-shocked if you turn them over as I did. Give it some time, or else you will be mopping up messes longer than you needed to. I mopped up messes for years before it stabilized. No one told me that I should retain the discipline of my children until they actually had some history and relationship with my new husband. Good advice. Heed it.

**5. I lived in my emotions.**

If you make your problems precious, they will poison you. Sometimes we do this with our emotions—we allow them to control us and move us in ways that don't honor God. Quit complaining about every little thing, and start praying about every little thing. Live in faith and not in emotions. It's a choice. It might be the hardest one you have made in a long time—but this choice goes a long way!

**6. I talked negatively about and behaved rudely to my children's parent and my stepchildren's parent.**

This is one of the most detrimental things we can do. Remember that the other half of your child is their other parent. So when you speak negatively about that parent, you are speaking negatively about the child, because they feel a part of that parent. Part of their identity comes from their connection to that parent. So behaving rudely toward the other parents hurts the children. Sometimes our hurt causes us to do stupid things. We need to learn to hold our tongues and pray.

**7. I was hurt, jealous, or petty over childish things with my stepchildren.**

I can remember that when one of my stepdaughters was about nine years old, she never wanted to touch me—I mean like in the game keep-away. Once she was passing me on the staircase, and she plastered herself against the wall with her arms spread out just to make sure I would not brush against her while we were passing. It hurt me so much, and it shocked me that I took a nine-year-old's actions so personally. But I went into my room and cried. There comes a point where you have to choose to look beyond and get over the things that hurting children do.

**8. I was mad at my husband because he was upset with my kids.**

Because I didn't know how to separate myself from my husband's feelings about my children's behavior, I internalized those feelings as if they were about me, and this caused many problems.

**9. I didn't realize that God had placed me in the life of this stepchild for His reasons.**

It's not about us; it's about a bigger picture. Someone has said, "A hundred years from now it will not matter what kind of car I drove, what kind of house I lived in, how much I've had in my bank account, or what my clothes looked like. What matters is that the world would be a better place, because I was important in the life of a child." God has placed us in the lives of our stepchildren. They might act like they hate you—they don't; they are just mixed up and hurt. Make a difference by accepting and loving them and by doing so embracing God's bigger picture.

**10. I refused to get better and stayed bitter.**

I can remember my mother calling the girls the "little princesses," and she didn't mean it in a nice Disney way. She was putting them down. I used to laugh at that comment, but then I realized it was only fueling my bitterness toward having to deal with kids who didn't want me in their lives. I was allowing the root of bitterness, and it had to stop. So I asked my mother never to call them that again and began speaking only a blessing toward them and praying for them daily. My attitude changed almost overnight. It was a choice.

## Moving beyond Myself

What has been necessary to move past myself? These four things:

1. Acceptance: living in the unexpected
2. Surrender: living with new challenges
3. Humility: living with new relationships
4. Higher-road living: living with new hope

*Acceptance:* This is your new reality. This is your new family. Learn to live in it, and learn to live in it well. In acceptance there comes peace. Jesus said, "In this world you will have trouble. But take heart! I have overcome the world" (John 16:33).

*Surrender:* To surrender is to relinquish possession. In order to surrender, we must remember who we are and *whose* we are. This has been the most important part of my personal change. To know that

I am His, and that my children are His, and that my stepchildren are His—this knowledge has opened me up to the idea that God wants to pour His love through me to the others in my life.

Surrender had to replace my stubbornness! I reminded myself:

- Present yourself to God as a living sacrifice (Rom. 12:1).
- Commit your way to Him (Ps. 37:5).
- Acknowledge Him in all your ways (Prov. 3:6).
- You are a people belonging to God (1 Peter 2:9).

*Humility:* Humility isn't being a doormat; it is simply bowing down before God, in heart and attitude. *What would You do here, Jesus? What would Your love, Your hands, look like in this situation?* I reminded myself:

- God opposes the proud and gives grace to the humble (James 4:6).
- Submit yourself to God and resist Satan (James 4:7).

*Higher-road living:* As Christians in stepfamilies, we must make a commitment to continue in our walk of faith, even in this family unit. I reminded myself:

- Turn the other cheek (Luke 6:29).
- Bless those who curse me (Luke 6:28).
- Give over and over (Luke 6:38).
- Forgive again and again (Luke 17:3–4).
- Offer grace (Luke 6:36).
- Live at peace when at all possible (Rom. 12:18).
- Don't demand your own way (Phil. 2:4).

Finally, if I could leave you with five key points, here they are:

1. Choose to have good working relationships.

2. Understand good, healthy boundaries that honor God.

3. Choose to see your stepchildren as people created and loved by God.

4. Remind yourself that hurting people hurt people, and pray for them.

5. Speak forgiveness talk. Look for the good. Dwell there.

## Bringing It Home

- What are the good things about your ex that you can focus on and teach to your children?
- When was the last time you were kind to your wife-in-law? Reflect on your feelings toward her, and decide what you want to do going forward.
- What is your top ten mistake list as of today?

# 11

# Becoming a New Kind of Dad

*Called to Be a Leader by Love and Example*

**Working smarter means understanding
the dynamics of stepfamily life
and development, and making
intentional decisions about how
you will grow together emotionally,
psychologically, and spiritually.**[1]

When I (Ray) became a father, I don't remember being handed a rule book or a role book. All I know is that nothing could have prepared me for the love I would have for my precious baby girls. In the same way, nothing could have prepared me for the pain of not raising them the way I had hoped—nor did I ever in my wildest dreams think I would be raising someone else's children while my children were tucked in each night thousands of miles away by another man living out my role as a father. Truth is, none of us get married hoping that someday our marriage will end in divorce and we will be relegated to the role of a part-time parent.

In record speed I had to learn how to become a daddy, and years later I had to learn how to become not only a new kind of dad to my own children, but a new kind of dad to Debbie's sons. Just as there wasn't a book to show step-by-step fathering skills, there isn't anything to teach me how to rise up to be the man I need to be in order to be a stepfather.

When your children live thousands of miles away from you, you need to learn new skills to connect with them, assure them of your love, and keep the relationship close. When you inherit children who are not your own, you need to learn how to connect with them on a level that is loving and nonthreatening.

## Facing Challenges with Courage

Here are some of the key challenges that being a new kind of dad brings with it.

For the biological father:

- Being away from your children—loss of relationship
- Feeling the need to make up for lost time when you are together
- Establishing a healthy co-parenting relationship with your former spouse
- Learning to share your parental influence with their stepfather
- Financial responsibilities as a result of divorce
- Accepting the fact that you have little or no

influence on what goes on at the other parent's home

For the stepfather:

- Feeling guilty about raising someone else's children while yours are not with you
- The struggle to figure out how you are to respond to the children, feel about them, and interact with them
- Feeling like a stranger in your own home
- Not having the same influence or respect that a natural father would have
- Allowing the biological parent to be the primary disciplinarian
- Accepting the fact that you will experience rejection, because stepchildren tend to remain loyal to their natural parents

I don't think any of us had any kind of an idea just how challenging our family would become once we got married. As I look back, I wish someone who had previously traveled this uncharted territory had shared some of the sobering realities we would soon face. God was going to teach all of us some important lessons about life that would challenge us to the core but in the end would be profitable beyond what we could have ever imagined.

The new life lessons presented in my new family have made me a better husband, a better father, and more importantly a more godly man—a man sensitive to God's leading. I have come to know that life is not about me. It never was and never will be. I have come to know that God has a perfect plan for my life and that my role is to simply trust Him. It is my sincere hope that you will be encouraged and will see that if you stay the course, the payoff is substantial. It certainly has been for me.

Two of the most frequently asked questions in blended-family marriages center on the question of loving someone else's children. Have you ever asked yourself:

- Why is it so hard to love another person's children?
- Why can't my spouse love my children?

The truth is, it is unnatural to love someone else's children, because we lack the biological bond that God intended we would experience in our nuclear families. This relational reality can become a constant source of conflict in blended families if we don't accept the fact that we are not related by blood. It's equally important that we accept that it is okay to feel the angst of the conflict.

But these facts don't relieve us as stepparents from the responsibility to lovingly provide for the physical and emotional needs of both our biological and nonbiological children, with the hope that over time we might become *love related* to our stepchildren.

## The High Calling to Love

No one should be pressured to manufacture feelings for another human being, but common decency dictates that we be open to a relationship built on mutual respect and a sense of responsibility for every member of the family. I have come to know that God has given me a high calling as a stepparent. He called me to love someone else's children as if they were my own. In God's view, whether those feelings come naturally or not is secondary to the fact that God has given me the unique privilege to be a godly influence in the lives of two wonderful young men who never wanted their parents to divorce, nor were ever given a voice in the decisions made.

I have also come to know that as much as I love my wife, the best gift I ever gave her was learning to love her two sons as if they were mine. There is nothing I wouldn't do for my stepsons that I would do for my daughters. In the middle of the struggles that exist in blended families, I have been given the precious gift that all of us want in life: the gift of being loved and giving love. I can honestly say that now more than ever, I understand the fact that God called me to a place of influence. God has called me to be a godly influence not just in my daughters' lives but also in my sons' lives. What a blessing I have been given!

I have also learned that there is nothing second class about being in a blended family. Admittedly, our blended family faces unique challenges, but in God's eyes there is nothing second best about our family. God as a loving Father continues to love us despite our failures. He is the God of second chances. His very nature is love. He chooses to love even those who do not love Him. God provides the strength we need to love others whom we find unlovable.

## My Role as a Stepfather

As a stepfather I struggled for years trying to understand my role in my sons' lives. Over the years, the question of just how I fit into their lives frequently surfaced. After all, I never wanted to replace their father. They had a dad they loved. As a result, I experienced what is best described as a low-grade discomfort that surfaced from time to time and caused me to keep my sons at arm's distance emotionally.

I coached their teams and was involved in their activities. But I have found myself continuously trying to figure out just exactly how I fit in as a parent and even felt concerned about how much fatherly influence I should exercise. These feelings are noteworthy, because it would not have been my nature to feel uncomfortable in my parental role.

I think for the most part these feelings are natural, and if I explore and understand them, I can have healthy relationships with my stepsons. Truth is, as bonded as I am and as much as I love my sons, this still remains a growth area for me. What ultimately guides me is my desire to be faithful to the calling God has given me in their lives. I truly believe I have been called as a stepparent, and what a blessing it is to love and provide for them physically, emotionally, and spiritually. In no way do I ever want to replace their dad, but I do understand that my role in their lives is a significant one I must willingly shoulder, even if at times it seems confusing.

As stepparents, we have been given a wonderful opportunity to influence our stepchildren's lives by modeling and teaching healthy values. We must understand that our children are watching our lives. Daily we are announcing to them what to value and how to live. If we want them to treasure the truth, then we must do so ourselves. If we live a lie, then we tell a lie.

Children are quick to see the hypocrisy in our lives. As stepparents we can become change agents by creating a safe place for them to share their feelings. To do so, it's critical we understand that it takes time to establish a trusting relationship with our stepchildren. It's dangerous to think that it won't require time and our personal attention to break through the barriers of their feelings of disloyalty to their biological father. We need to go slowly and spend as much one-on-one time with our stepchildren as possible in order to build a relationship of trust. If your stepchildren choose to reject you, just know that their feelings are normal.

## My Role as a Biological Father

God hates divorce (Mal. 2:16). Divorce is the ripping apart of a family that was once bonded by a godly covenant. Divorce does end a marriage, but it should not end a family. When a couple divorces, the children do not. They remain the constant connection between their divorced parents. One of the challenges we face in becoming a new kind of dad centers on how to remain actively and emotionally connected to our biological children if we don't have sole custody.

How do we continue to have the parental significance that we want to have and that our children need us to have when we become part-time parents? This is a real challenge, particularly in situations where divorce poison has settled in as the result of a bitter court battle. The problem of maintaining an intimate bond with our children must be addressed, or we face the likelihood of losing our children's affection and the ability to lovingly influence their lives.

Too often, time, distance, and parental alienation can influence a dad to check out. On some level I battled the emotions of giving up. I battled whether or not I would ever have the kind of influence on my daughters that I wanted to have. It's difficult to be a part-time parent and even more difficult to be a long-distance parent. In the depth of my heart I understood that if I was ever going to have the

significance I wanted, and that they needed from me, I was going to
have to stay connected to them.

They needed to know that the love that I had for them was secure
and that I was every bit as committed to them as I was before they
moved away. They needed to know that I would be there for them at
all times, no matter the circumstances.

I could not allow myself to dwell negatively on the circumstances that I found myself in. The Enemy of our faith wants us to
check out. To run from our fatherly responsibilities. I knew that my
daughters needed me to stay the course and to remain fully engaged,
no matter what the obstacles. I had to be intentional about staying in
contact with them. That meant frequent phone calls. It meant trying
to consciously walk in their shoes. It meant a desire to understand
their world while sharing mine. It meant being excited about their
activities, their friends, and their experiences. It meant helping them
feel safe to openly share their lives without a concern that it would
hurt me because of the separation. It meant assuring them repeatedly
that all of us in California loved them and missed them. As much as
I missed them, I had to communicate to them that I was happy for
them.

I have to admit there were times when I could sense a disconnect with the girls when they came to visit for the holidays and
summer vacations. We always went through a warming-up period
as we settled in for another visit. We were always excited to see one
another, and the reunions at the airport were always wonderful and
filled with anticipation about our time together as a family. We
went out of our way to lovingly greet my daughters and to prepare
our home for their visits so they would know they were loved. I

don't think there was ever a time when I did not greet them with flowers.

But as high as the reunions were for me, the send-offs were equally painful. At times I became tearful as I said my good-byes, because I knew it would be several months before I would see them again. Debbie frequently commented that, for days after Ashley and Megan left, there was a sense of sadness about me. But I could never embrace the fact that they weren't with me more. Over time I did my best to channel the disappointment at their leaving by having a grateful heart for the time that we had been together. In doing so, I think it made it easier for them to leave.

We simply learned to cherish the time together and to accept the realities of our relationship. I think unconsciously we learned to accept and appreciate that the distance and the infrequency of our visits could not change the fact that we loved one another.

## Trusting That God Is in Control

As a new kind of dad, I had to learn to trust and fully rely on the fact that God was in control. I could no longer trust in myself. The once self-protective, defensive behavior patterns that I displayed when relationally threatened were no longer acceptable. I began to accept there was a better way. I had to trust Him with every aspect of my life.

I had to decide to package up the hurt of an unwanted divorce and the pain of being separated from my children and begin to appreciate God's provision. I had to become comfortable with things that I had little or no control of. In doing so, I became more appreciative of the blessings that God had so richly lavished on both me and my family.

## My Stepchildren Needed Me

I had loved Debbie from the very beginning, but I had not completely accepted my role in my sons' lives. I became more accepting of the fact that God had placed me in a position of influence with my stepsons. I began to better understand the importance of my influence on them. My love for them grew, because I could finally see that God was calling me to love them just as if they were my biological sons—and, more importantly, as He loved them.

They needed me to be the godly man that Christ was calling me to be. Once I accepted that fact, my relationship with the boys began to dramatically change. As I look back, I see the precious gift that I have been given in being a stepfather to two amazing young men.

As a father and as a stepparent, I have made numerous mistakes along the way. I am grateful for God's grace and forgiveness. There were times when my pride got in the way. I remember the kids frequently saying to me when there were disagreements, "Dad, why do you always have to be right?" Of course, my response was to always defend myself.

I have come to understand that very often the people who find the need to argue or justify their position are the ones probably the most wrong. As a new kind of dad, I have come to know that there is power in an apology. God has truly humbled my heart.

I now realize that although I never set out to fail my children, I have and I will. God has not called me to be perfect, nor has He called you to be perfect. He has, however, called us into a personal relationship with Him that requires us to be sensitive to His leading. As I reflect back, I wish I had realized early on the need to surrender my will to His.

It is my sincere hope that as a stepparent you will come to a place of victory, if you have not already done so, where you can joyfully accept the call of God on your life.

## Bringing It Home

- Do you see your role as a father as a calling from God? What are the implications of that?
- Do you believe that you are in your stepchild's life for God's purposes? How does what you believe about this affect what you do?
- As a man, can you admit you make mistakes? If so, what are some of those?
- What do you think of the term "the power of an apology"?
- Is there anyone you need to apologize to?

# Ever After

*Loving God and Loving Others
Is All That Really Counts*

**It has been said that, "You don't marry
one person; you marry three: The person
you think they are, the person they are,
and the person they are going to become
as the result of being married to you."**

Richard Needham

We have spent significant time talking about the wedding, the expectations, and the death of the dream. We have also talked about the foundations of loss and the pitfalls of all the blended-family dynamics. Now we would like to conclude with the charge to make sure, above all else, that the marriage is cultivated for growth.

The rules and roles of the second marriage are very much the same as those the first time around. A man desires respect, and a woman desires love. In his book *Love and Respect*, author Emerson

Eggerichs spells out how we can learn to live in a different way toward our spouse. In fact there are many fine marriage books on the market, and we encourage you to pick up a book or two, read them, and discuss how you can continue growing and building your marriage relationship. Some of our favorite authors are Bill and Pam Farrel, H. Norman Wright, Gary Thomas, Les and Leslie Parrott, Gary Smalley, Ted Cunningham, and Gary Oliver.

One thing for sure, marriage is more than a courtship and wedding. Marriage is a commitment to another person, and in a remarriage it is commitment to the other person as well as a commitment to their children. We especially like the term Gary Thomas uses: *sacred marriage.*

In their book *The Way of Agape,* authors Chuck and Nancy Missler lead the reader to learn what it means to walk in God's love in our relationships with other people. We highly recommend this, as God's love is the only thing that will take your marriage through the ups and downs of real life. Without an understanding of the power of God's love living through us, we have to love in our own strength and on our own terms.

The experts say that to have a healthy marriage we need:

- Healthy expectations
- A realistic concept of love
- A positive attitude toward life
- The ability to communicate our feelings
- An understanding and acceptance of our gender differences
- The ability to make decisions and settle arguments
- A common spiritual foundation and goal

And for those marrying a second time around with kids from their first marriage, there are a couple of additional characteristics:

- Knowledge of what it takes to combine a family
- Stepparenting skills
- Willingness to see loving our stepchild as a gift from God and a call from God

Ron Deal says,

> A strong remarriage is critical for the relational development of the children. Stepfamily children, especially those who have lived through a parental divorce, need to witness and learn from a healthy marital relationship. This counteracts the negative and destructive patterns of interaction they witnessed in their parents' previous marriage (and since the divorce). Children desperately need positive marital role models. If not, they are likely to repeat destructive relationship patterns. Indeed, children of divorce have a much higher risk of divorce in their own adult relationships. However, positive relationship models can counteract destructive ones.[1]

## Two Working Together

Building a lasting marriage does not just happen. It's a lifelong commitment of two people working diligently together. Here are some of the principles that have been helpful for us:

- Date for a lifetime.

- Compliment your partner daily.
- Frequently tell your mate you love them.
- Ideally, husbands and wives are best friends as well as lovers.
- Spend time together. For many, love is spelled TIME. Love is not self-sustaining.
- Listen with a third ear.
- Practice unconditional acceptance. The deepest kind of sharing can take place only when there is no fear of rejection.
- Focus on what is wrong, not who is wrong.
- Focus on commonalities. Intimacy grows when nurtured by shared emotions, experiences, and beliefs.
- Explore and experience spiritual intimacy together.
- Strive to meet your spouse's needs.
- Make your commitment part of your daily being. As humans we create and define ourselves through our commitments.
- Be sensitive to God's leading. Recognize that ultimately, God is in control.
- Be civil to your ex-spouse. It is important that you complete the unfinished business from your first marriage if you want to succeed in your second. Come to terms with your past.
- Have empathy for your spouse in the stepparent role. Recognize that the biological parent is more likely to be tolerant of a child's behavior.

- Start slow, go slow, build relationship.
- Give your spouse time alone with their biological children.
- Make your marriage the first priority.
- Make new marriage traditions.
- Understand that in the best marriages there are difficulties.

Probably the biggest thing for us was learning to meet in the middle. "Not right, not wrong—just different" was our slogan. In order to do this, we had to first come to a place of wanting to honor each other and the relationship. Then we had to humbly submit ourselves to the formation of the relationship. Next we had to quit assuming our way was the right way, and be open and receptive to our spouse. This simple practice has changed everything.

Jesus Christ gave very clear, albeit hard, instructions for human relationships. These instructions are for dealing with people who might not be treating us in the way we hoped. We believe that these things are exactly what Jesus would do if He were dealing with others in the blended family today:

> But I tell you who hear me: Love
> your enemies, do good to those who
> hate you, bless those who curse you,
> pray for those who mistreat you.... 
> Do to others as you would have
> them do to you.... Be merciful,
> just as your Father is merciful.
> Do not judge, and you will not be

*judged…. Forgive, and you will be*
*forgiven. Give, and it will be given*
*to you. (Luke 6:27–28, 31, 36–38)*

Memorize these eight bullets and apply them to your relationship with your spouse, stepchildren, ex-spouses:

- Love
- Do good
- Bless
- Pray for
- Be merciful toward
- Do not judge
- Forgive
- Give

With God, all things are possible! And when things get rocky, you must be committed to doing your part. Paul wrote,

*If it is possible, as far as it depends on*
*you, live at peace with everyone. Do*
*not take revenge…. On the contrary:*
*"If your enemy is hungry, feed him;*
*if he is thirsty, give him something to*
*drink." (Rom. 12:18–20)*

So how do we live happily ever after, even after broken promises, broken dreams, and bruised lives? By returning again and again to the Father and following His way, the way of love and the narrow, uncommon road that leads to peace.

# Notes

*Introduction: Happily Ever After—Again?*
1. C. S. Lewis (letter to Sheldon Vanauken), quoted in Sheldon Vanauken, *A Severe Mercy* (San Francisco: HarperOne, 1987), 134.

*Chapter 1: Once upon a Dream ...*
1. Barbara LeBey, *Remarried with Children* (New York: Bantam, 2005), 4.

2. Ron Deal, *The Smart Stepfamily* (Bloomington, MN: Bethany House, 2002), 24.

3. LeBey, *Remarried with Children*, 1.

*Chapter 2: Who Are We?*
1. Ron Deal and Laura Petherbridge, *The Smart Stepmom* (Bloomington, MN: Bethany House, 2009), 21.

2. *Webster's II New Riverside Dictionary*, s.v. "Blend."

3. Adapted from Maxine Marsolini, *Blended Families* (Chicago: Moody, 2000), 11.

4. LeBey, *Remarried with Children*, 25.

5. Joseph Warren Kniskern, *When the Vow Breaks* (Nashville, TN: Broadman and Holman, 1993), 248.

*Chapter 3: Learning to Live with New Hope*
1. *Webster's New American Dictionary*, s.v. "Hope."

2. Max Lucado, *Hope Pure and Simple* (Nashville, TN: Nelson, 2007),17.

3. Ibid., 61.

4. Kniskern, *When the Vow Breaks,* 256.

*Chapter 4: These Families Are Different*
1. Tom Worthen, ed., *Broken Hearts ... Healing: Young Poets Speak Out on Divorce,* 19, quoted in Deal, *The Smart Stepfamily,* 112.

2. James H. Bray and John Kelly, *Stepfamilies: Love, Marriage, and Parenting in the First Decade* (New York: Broadway, 1998), 8.

3. Ibid.

4. LeBey, *Remarried with Children,* 23–24.

5. Adapted from Angela Elwell Hunt, *Loving Someone Else's Child* (Nashville, TN: Tyndale, 1992), 223.

*Chapter 5: The Power of the Biological Bond*
1. Dr. Donald Partridge and Jenetha Partridge, *Loving Your Stepfamily* (Pleasanton, CA: Institute for Family Research and Education, 2007), 15.

2. Ibid., 11.

3. Susan Hetrick, *Advice from the Blender* (Longwood, FL: Xulon Press, 2007), 21–22.

4. Partridge and Partridge, *Loving Your Stepfamily,* 13.

*Chapter 6: The New Home Front*
1. LeBey, *Remarried with Children*, 23

2. *Webster's New Collegiate Dictionary*, s.v. "Discipline."

3. Partridge and Partridge, *Loving Your Stepfamily*, 71.


*Chapter 7: Attention to Details*
1. Used with permission.

2. Patricia Lowe, *The Cruel Stepmother* (Englewood Cliffs, NJ: Prentice Hall, 1970).

3. LeBey, *Remarried with Children*, 171–172.


*Chapter 8: Children Matter*
1. Marsolini, *Blended Families*, 116.

2. Deal and Petherbridge, *The Smart Stepmom*, 66.

3. H. Norman Wright, *It's Okay to Cry: A Parent's Guide to Helping Children Through the Losses of Life* (Colorado Springs, CO: WaterBrook, 2004), 17–26; referenced in Deal and Petherbridge, *The Smart Stepmom*, 72.

4. Deal and Petherbridge, *The Smart Stepmom*, 74–75.

5. Dr. Richard Warshak, *Divorce Poison* (San Francisco: Regan Books, 2003), 5.

6. Ibid., 14.

7. Ibid., 127.

8. Laura Sherman Walters, *There's a New Family in My House!*, quoted in Marsolini, *Blended Families*, 127.

9. Marsolini, *Blended Families*, 108.

10. Ibid., 109.

*Chapter 9: From the Other Side*
1. Lucado, *Hope Pure and Simple,* 118.

*Chapter 10: Help! I'm the Mom in This Mess*
1. Beth Moore, "Difficulty," in *A Quick Word with Beth Moore: Scriptures and Quotations from Breaking Free* (Nashville, TN: Broadman and Holman, 2008).

2. Used with permission.

3. Used with permission.

*Chapter 11: Becoming a New Kind of Dad*
1. Deal, *The Smart Stepfamily,* 12.

*Ever After*
1. Deal, *The Smart Stepfamily,* 26.

*At our wedding, 1990*

*Celebrating in Maui, 2008*

For more information about living
life in the blended family or to
have Ray and Debbie do a Blended
Family Seminar or speaking
engagement, contact them at:

www.blendedfamilyliving.com

JOHN 14 4-5

1 JOHN 1-9.

MATTHEW 6:34

JEREMIAH 33-3

ROMANS 12: 9-21